DEPENDANCE

vs

OPPORTUNITY...

a cycle that CAN be broken

Paul McKessy

Contents

Dedication 5

1 From Youth to Youth Worker 1

2 Sure Beats Stacking Bricks! 19

3 In Search of Self 39

4 Back into it 45

5 Passion vs Fear 69

6 Let the Games Begin 87

7 So What Now? 115

8 Spotlight on Youth 127

9 Going National 139

10 Success Was Not Enough 153

11 One Door Closes 161

12 So what's next? 185

Dedication

This book is dedicated to my wife Sharon Kosmina, my two sons Jordan and David and the 1200 or more young people, the staff, hundreds of volunteers, employers, benefactors and mums and dads who were either inspired or desperate enough to be part of the Breaking the Cycle project proving without a shadow of a doubt the premise "if you give young people regardless of their past the skills and opportunity they will muster the desire and motivation to be far more powerful than they or most people ever dreamt possible and go on to live out their life's ambition."

About This Book

"Paul's conversational approach to his life journey is refreshing in its honesty and demonstrates why he was so well placed to become "part of the solution" at Breaking the Cycle. His courage and in the trenches attitude to really batting for young people is heart warming. To see in person the graduations and the transformations through that time I can truly say this was real progress and life changing for so many people. The learnings are as relevant today as we see a rise in depression and more prisons being built. An inspiring read for anyone who wishes to see a better future for our young people."

Karen Knowles,
International Recording Artist

When I was approached by Paul McKessy about employing a bunch of homeless and long term unemployed kids i admit i had my reservations but fortunately i listened to my instincts and thank goodness I did.
I was so impressed with the quality of program and the raw talent and desire to succeed of the young graduates I joined the Board of Directors of Breaking the Cycle and Spotlight went on to employ more than 200 Breaking the Cycle graduates some of whom are still with the company some 20 years later.
Dependance Vs Opportunity is a page turning recall of what is possible when young people from any background are given the appropriate opportunity, challenge, skills and support and a must read for any employers wanting to increase the social responsibility and workforce culture of their organisation.

Morry Fraid,
Executive Chairman, Spotlight Group Holdings

1
From Youth to Youth Worker

When I stop to think about it, I have either been a young person or worked with young people almost all of my life. In 1979, at the ripe old age of nineteen, I was employed as a professional youth worker, with no qualifications other than my enthusiasm and ability to communicate with other young people. That wasn't hard – I was one.

It wasn't a particularly well-thought-out career path. I had left school at fifteen to work as an apprentice motor mechanic with Sunicrust Bakeries. I didn't like the job much, and I was possibly the worst motor mechanic ever to enter the industry. The job did serve its purpose, though. It got me out of school. I hated school with a passion.

I couldn't see any point whatsoever in attending school, apart from having the opportunity to play football and meet my friends. My results reflected my effort. It wasn't as if I was stupid – quite the contrary. I just couldn't for the life of me see how school had any relevance to me. Not that I had any clues about what was relevant. I was screaming to be independent, and I wasn't happy about being told what to do by really old people – the teachers.

Unearned respect for authority was not one of my strong suits then, nor is it today. So at fifteen, knowing everything there was to know about life – all of which, incidentally, I have subsequently forgotten – I confronted my parents with the fact that I wanted to leave school.

Now, my parents were great people. There was no local high school in Craigieburn, the new northern suburb of Melbourne where we lived, so at great personal sacrifice my parents had sent me to a Catholic boarding school in Sunbury, about 15 kilometres away. Was I grateful? Appreciative of their effort and pride in providing me with the best education they could afford? Hardly.

When I started secondary school, I was a bright, enthusiastic, energetic kid who in many ways could do no wrong. I was popular, had lots of friends and lived to play football. I had been in the top 1 or 2 per cent academically at my primary school, and life was good. I sat the entrance exam for the boarding school, scored a respectable result and was placed in the class for the academically 'bright' students. We studied Latin, Italian and Maths 1 and 2. The not so academically 'bright' students did woodwork and metalwork.

My first year of high school was a profound learning experience, but my learning had very little to do with the classroom. It was far more to do with surviving injustice, fear and abuse. Being smaller than most kids my age and having carrot-red hair, I was a prime target for the school bullies, who were there in large numbers.

Until then, I had never experienced being systematically beaten up for no apparent reason other than that I was in the wrong place at the wrong time. I had no-one to protect me, because if you went to the brothers you were dead meat. I was eleven years old, away from the safety, security and protection of home, and not a day passed without my being punched, spat on, kicked – or, worst of all, laughed at. In short, my life was hell.

I didn't feel able to tell anyone, particularly my parents, who thought they were doing their very best to give me the education they didn't have. Many years later, I realised how important those years were in forming my beliefs and values about what was and what was not OK. Without that experience, my life could have taken a very different direction. Instead of escaping school as quickly as I did, I might have sailed through twelve years of schooling, gone on to university and become a lawyer – or, God forbid, a politician.

I was a classic case: the kid with huge potential, 'failing' Year 9 Maths and English. By Year 9, I was well and truly doing woodwork, where my only claim to fame was taking two terms to finish a pencil case with a lid that didn't fit. So, at the age of fifteen and a half, I summoned the courage to tell Mum and Dad that I wanted to leave school. Naturally, they were very disappointed, but to their credit they said if that was what I really wanted to do then they would let me leave school. There was only one proviso. I had to have a job to go to. I remember it well. That was on a Thursday night, and I started work with Sunicrust Bakeries the following Monday.

For the first time in my life I began to get a sense that I could make my life the way I wanted it to be. If there was something I was unhappy with, the only person who could do anything about it was me. The only trouble was that, like most 15-year-olds, I didn't have a clue how I *DID* want my life to be. I was clear about what I didn't want, though, and felt pleased with myself for being able to take charge. I was one of the first kids in my peer group to leave school and begin mixing it with the 'grown-ups'. Having independence and a little bit of money was a great experience, and I was soon able to do far more things that I wanted to do.

As I said, I was a shocking motor mechanic, and it would be fair to say the men I was working with were not particularly gifted when it came to providing a 'positive learning environment'. My self-confidence at work was not high, but as a result of my experiences at school, I had developed some excellent strategies for handling intimidation, so when I was on the receiving end of uncomplimentary remarks, it was like water off a duck's back.

After a couple of years, a familiar pattern began to emerge. I became restless and spent most of my time being dissatisfied. I decided I was not cut out to be a motor mechanic, so – much to my boss's delight – I changed jobs within the company and began delivering bread. This didn't last long, because the hours were definitely not conducive to being eighteen and having a social life. After three and a half years, which at that age seemed an eternity, I left Sunicrust and began a new career as a brick stacker at the Clifton Brickworks.

Yet again, I had the experience of being dissatisfied and doing something about it. Some people say I'm blessed. Others say I am just a tinny bugger. I don't know what it is, but about two weeks after I started at Clifton Brick, one of the bricklayers' labourers was sick. A manager came up to where I was standing among fifteen or twenty others and pointed to me. 'You, come with me.' Not knowing what I'd done wrong, I followed him rather nervously to the other side of the factory, where the bricklayers were. The manager said to a brickie, 'Here's ya new labourer.' From brick stacker to labourer in two weeks – was there no limit to what this boy could do?

The next day, the company announced it was shutting down one of the kilns and all the brick stackers who had been employed in the last six months were to be laid off at the end of the week. Of the fifteen or twenty blokes I had been standing with, twelve were let go. But me, I was a brickie's labourer!

Again I learnt a valuable lesson. Whenever anyone in the factory was sick, I would volunteer to do their job while they were away, often on top of my own job. Within about twelve months I could operate almost every machine in the place, and I had made myself as indispensable as possible.

Life at the brickworks suited me quite well – great money, plenty of overtime, start early, finish early. It was a good job, or so I thought.

Whenever I wasn't working I would hang about with my mates, usually down at the local shops. I didn't realise that groups of fifteen or twenty frisky teenagers could intimidate some people by their mere presence. Though I couldn't see it, in the eyes of some we constituted a 'gang', which at the time was not a term of affection.

Occasionally there would be a fight or someone would be drunk, but mostly we were just a bunch of local kids hanging around the shops for lack of anywhere else to meet.

I didn't get heavily into the gang scene, but several times I happened to be present when a 'gang of youths', as the newspapers would describe them, came up from Broadmeadows to beat the stuffing out of us. Broadmeadows was a working-class suburb six miles south of us, directly down the Hume Highway, and was notorious for being a particularly rough area. Some rude people use to say that Broadmeadows was the arsehole of the world, and Craigieburn was six miles up it.

By this time, I had experienced quite enough beatings, so when faced with the choice of being beaten or doing the beating, I chose the latter. Not that I often got the choice.

Honestly, it was crazy. I had my first experience of this when for no apparent reason six or eight cars appeared from nowhere and twenty or thirty kids jumped out and came racing toward us, swinging pipes and baseball bats. I couldn't believe my eyes. It was like a scene out of an American cop show – no doubt a source of inspiration to many.

In my naivety, I stepped to the front of the pack, obviously unarmed, and appealed for calm. Surprisingly, it worked. After yelling abuse and insults, the would-be bashers got back in their car and screeched off. I repeated my performance a couple of times. Then, one day, one of the kids behind me started yelling abuse back. Now, this was not a good look. If I could have gotten to the kid behind me before they did, I would have thumped him. Straight away, it was on for young and old – and I was at the front of the pack. It wasn't a pretty sight.

This was the stuff the papers make a meal of. Thirty or forty brawling youths, shop windows smashed – it was a serious affray. (Not that I knew what an 'affray' was until later, when the police read out some of the charges.)

There were people everywhere – girls giving out high-pitched screams, yells and insults, packs of four or five boys kicking the life out of some poor unfortunate who had fallen to the ground. Beer bottles were hurled at bodies and through windows. There were bats, cricket stumps, knuckle-dusters, garden stakes – you name it. People used any weapon in reach. I still don't know how someone wasn't killed.

This was my first real introduction to gang warfare as it was in the late '70s and early '80s in Melbourne. Alienated young people were beginning to do the only thing they knew how to do in order to exert a little bit of power. Unfortunately, it was usually at the expense of another group of alienated young people, and so was not particularly useful in the big picture. It was kids lashing out at anyone or anything they could.

Looking back now, I can see it was like a collective temper tantrum at not getting what you wanted or felt you deserved: a job, respect, a bright future. For many of these young people, there was no place in society. Schools didn't want them, employers didn't want them, clubs of various sorts didn't understand them or meet their needs. So they went about creating identities and networks where they did feel understood, where they were accepted for who they were, where they belonged and experienced mateship and support. They found this in their gangs.

Like most institutions, each gang had its rules, policies, procedures, hierarchy and culture. The gangs that I had dealings with were usually very controlling, but at least you belonged somewhere and if you stuck together you were afforded protection against the other gangs, for what it was worth.

Over a period of about six or eight months, I witnessed half a dozen of these big fights. Though I was only eighteen years old, I was absolutely buggered if I could see the sense in it. Partly I was scared of being beaten up or killed, but I could also see it was a complete waste of energy. In a raw sense, this was to become my early 'training' ground for working with young people.

It was about this time that I met a crazy group of Christians who had taken it on themselves to set up a 'Christmas Mission' for teenagers in my home town. Given that there wasn't much else competing for our time, I thought it was worth investigating this mob, who had set up 'shop' in our footy changing rooms.

Having been brought up a Roman Catholic, I had never met Christians before. Since leaving school, I had not really considered the link between the church and Christianity. In fact, I had seen very little evidence to suggest there was one. You went to church because you were Catholic, not because of any significant belief or faith in God. It would be fair to say that I had rejected the church at this stage of my life. The decision was made easier by the fact that the bloke who collected my twenty cents from the plate at church on Sunday was the same bloke I had paid $5 to get into the porno night at the football club the previous Thursday.

But there was something very weird about these Christians at the 'mission'. They were all so bloody cheerful and genuinely happy. They were led by a bloke who was in his late thirties, which was pretty old as far as I was concerned. He dressed in army greens and Blundstone boots, long before the boots were a fashion statement. His name was Peter Chapman. When I met him, I had no inkling of the influence he would have on my life.

Peter was as straight as an arrow, with a short-back-and-sides and a military-type moustache. We kids, on the other hand, would have been more comfortable with the Woodstock genre or Sunbury '73, with Billy Thorpe and the Aztecs. I was very intrigued by these people, especially Peter, who for some unknown reason had a genuine interest in our lives. Must be suspect, I thought.

Peter Chapman was the first youth worker I had ever met. Until this point, I didn't know youth work existed – and in many ways it didn't, other than in a youth club-type environment. But what this crowd did to our footy sheds was unbelievable. From the fishnet draped beneath the blue fluorescent tubes to the false hessian walls and the sea-grass matting on the floor, this was not the home of the mighty Craigieburn Football Club that I had grown up with. Every night they had live musos singing good stuff. It was cool, in a daggy sort of way. It was certainly not what any of us kids in Craigieburn had ever experienced. The coffee shop served cinnamon toast, raisin toast, tea, coffee and cordial, all at a token price, and the great thing about the blue fluorescent lights was that if any of the girls wore white you could look through their tops and see their bras. I am not sure if this was sanctioned as part of the Christians' marketing strategy, but it worked for me.

I was quite capable of falling in love with a new girl every day, but at this coffee shop I found one who liked *ME*, a beautiful young woman called Jane Christie.

It was the Christmas holidays and the brickworks had closed for the break, so I had lots of time on my hands. The thought of going somewhere for a holiday would never have occurred to me. It was just a time to catch up with my mates, many of whom were still at school. I was intrigued by the Christians, and especially by their happiness. Most of us kids suspected that they were all smoking dope, even though we knew they wouldn't be.

It was a great summer. Jane and I fell in love, we had entertainment on tap, and there were new and interesting people to check out.

Getting to know Theo's Team, as they were called, broadened my horizons in many ways. The team members came from places like Eltham, Warrandyte, Strathmore and Blackburn. I had hardly heard of these places, let alone met anyone from there. It was my first exposure to middle-class people, and guess what? They were really nice.

The holidays passed and Theo's bugged out and the footy club got back to running the illegal gambling and porno nights commonly known as pre-season training. I was left feeling curious. Who were those people? I always suspected there was more to life than I had experienced to date, and I wanted to check it out.

At various times Pete Chapman had invited some of us to come along to the Friday night drop-in centre in Broadmeadows known as 'Theo's Broady'. Hang on a minute, I thought. The only contact I'd had with people from Broadmeadows was with the lunatics we had fought with at the Craigieburn shops – and Jane Christie. Bugger it, I'll go.

The centre consisted of two medium-sized rooms, one with some old dilapidated furniture and the other with a pool table. Off to the side was a small kitchenette. The kids who frequented the place were from Olsen Place, a small shopping strip around the corner from the drop-in centre, which was located in Camp Road.

Theo's Broady was a madhouse, and the maddest of the lot were the Christians who volunteered to 'staff' the place, week in and week out. Every Friday night, about fifteen or twenty teenage boys would come in, create havoc, half-wreck the place, abuse the Christians – often assaulting one or other of them – and leave. Then the Christians would sit around in a circle and pray for the kids.

Now, I was far from being an expert in youth affairs, but in my model of the world this was bordering on complete bloody insanity. I could not believe these fundamentally good people would tolerate this over and over again. They genuinely cared about these kids as if they were their own. As for me, I was in no man's land. The Olsen Place guys thought I was a Christian, the Christians were praying for me too, and me, well, I was completely confused.

One night the kids' behaviour was particularly unacceptable. Someone had set fire to the curtains, someone else had shat in a corner, and the tension was palpable. Then it blew. A full-scale fight broke out. One of the kids punched a friend of mine, so I stepped in. Despite my 5' 2" stature, I put this kid up against the wall and threatened to beat the shit out of him if he ever considered doing anything like it again. 'And that goes for the rest of you as well!' I screamed.

After about three seconds of silence, it dawned on me that this was not the smartest thing I had ever done. It could have gone either way. One of them walked toward me in an obviously threatening manner. At that moment the undisputed leader of the group, a mad Yugoslav called Drago Komjonovic, stepped in and said, 'Leave him alone. He's all right.' That was when I realised I was going to live. My respect in the place was established.

Drago was an amazing kid. Most people, including his mates, were justifiably scared of him. He was built like a brick shelter shed, with a big round face that could emit the fiercest of looks or the most radiant smiles. He had a look of Muhammad Ali, and could fight like him too.

One night, soon after that incident, I was buying milk and bread at the Olsen Place shops, which was an intimidating experience if you didn't know the locals, and I stopped to talk with Drago and a couple of the guys for a while. My timing could not have been worse. About four cars pulled up and out jumped twenty or so kids, all wielding weapons of one kind or another. It was a rival gang known as the Lebanese Tigers, who had made the trip across Broadmeadows from Dallas, where they occupied a shopping centre as their territory.

Here we go, I thought. Most of our guys took off, which was an acceptable thing to do, given the numbers. I didn't get away, so I did whatever I had to do to stay alive. But it was Drago that the Tigers were after. Someone stabbed him in the side, but, rather than fall to the ground and probably be kicked to death, Drago did something that still astounds me to this day. He picked up a metal rubbish bin that was chained to its holder, yanked the bin away, snapping the mooring, and proceeded to belt half a dozen or so attackers with the bin.

At this, the Tigers took off. As they drove away, Drago pitched the bin through the back window of the departing Valiant, shouting 'Gutless bastards!', then sat down in a pool of his own blood.

Before long there were police everywhere. Drago was carted off to the Royal Melbourne Hospital, where he made a full recovery in about a month. I went in to visit him in hospital, and he was genuinely grateful that I had stuck by him. He reckoned he would have been killed for sure if I hadn't.

I said, 'That's OK, mate, I owed you one.' But the truth was, I didn't really get the chance to run. I was too caught up in it, and in hindsight I am glad.

This event further increased my esteem among the Olsen Place boys, and as always Peter Chapman was keen to encourage me to get more involved in the work he was doing in Broadmeadows. As far as I was concerned, Peter was a very strange bloke, but I had the utmost respect for him and what he was doing. Virtually everyone else had written these 'Broady kids' off as a dead loss. Yet Peter and his small team of volunteers would do whatever they could to offer them some love and support. In some cases it was more than the kids had ever experienced from home. Peter never pushed Christianity much; he preferred to demonstrate his faith, not talk about it.

One evening Peter and I had a long rave and he asked me some pretty confronting questions.

'What do you want to do with your life, Paul?'

'I dunno,' I said.

'You know,' he continued, 'you are an amazing young man and you have got enormous potential to make a difference to the lives of a lot of kids who could really do with it. In life you can either be part of the solution or part of the problem. What is it going to be for you?'

'Hell, I don't know! What can I do?' I replied.

Peter asked me whether I would consider getting into youth work full-time.

It would sure beat the hell out of stacking bricks, I thought. That is still my yardstick when considering any occupation.

Jane and I were seriously in love, and we were planning to get married later in the year. Well, we were both nineteen now, and obviously very grown up! Jane had just completed Year 12, and she said she would take a job as a checkout chick at Coles or K-Mart to support us both if I went back to school to complete my education. I will always be in debt to Jane for that, and for encouraging me to be more than I thought I could be. So that was it. I decided I would go back to school, go to university and get a degree in youth work.

In some ways, it was pretty simple. Although I'd failed Year 9 and left school early, I found a secondary school, Moreland High School, that would accept me into their Year 12 Alternative Course STC. It wasn't the traditional HSC course, but it was enough for me to get into youth work if I passed. I hadn't looked at a book since I had left school – and, come to think about it, I hadn't done so then either – so to say I was apprehensive about returning to school would be an understatement. But it was a fabulous experience.

Because I was nineteen years old and by now married to Jane, I was considered a mature-age student. In many ways, I was able to bridge the gap between the other students and the staff. My being at Moreland High School really worked for everyone, including the teachers.

Moreland was piloting a new alternative year 12 for students who were not as academically strong or for those who wanted to complete their education but would have been unlikely to survive the traditional HSC. I was very clear why I was there: I was there to pass, in order to go on and do youth work at uni. Being there was costing me a year's wages as well. My motivation helped to inspire some of the other students, setting up a dynamic that proved useful for us all. I completed the year with flying colours, passing English, Economics, Media Studies, History and Environmental Science. I wondered what had happened in the five years since I left school the first time. Had I miraculously grown a brain?

Once more, good fortune was about to intercede in my life. I had applied to get into the Diploma of Youth Work at Phillip Institute, which shared a boundary wall with Pentridge Prison, when suddenly there was an explosion of youth-work jobs available. Youth unemployment had begun to surface as a serious issue for the first time since the 1930s, and the federal government had introduced a national program called the Community Youth Support Scheme (or CYSS, as it was more commonly known). While I was waiting for my interview at Phillip Institute, both Peter Chapman and Jane independently suggested I apply for a job as a CYSS project officer or youth worker. If I got one, great; if not, I would go on and do youth work at uni.

With assistance from Jane (she wrote the applications), I applied for several jobs in various Melbourne suburbs. I was able to draw on my own experience as a youth – I was still nineteen – and my voluntary work in Broadmeadows. One day I strolled out to the letterbox to find three letters addressed to me. I had been offered three jobs, all on the same day. One was in Broadmeadows, one in St Albans – another depressed area in the west of Melbourne, much like Broady – and one in Eltham, a leafy middle-class suburb in the east, renowned for its bushland, art and mud-brick houses.

I was in a quandary. What was I going to do?

Jane was very clear. 'Don't be stupid. We're going to Eltham.' And we did.

2
Sure Beats Stacking Bricks!

All things considered, the move to Eltham was a fairly smooth transition. It was probably made easier by my bright orange afro hairstyle, which seemed to be less conspicuous in Eltham than among the skinheads and 'sharps' of Broadmeadows. Jane and I moved into a rented house in the middle of town, then later shared a farmhouse on ten acres with two other people, ten minutes drive from Eltham. The farmhouse was tiny and very dilapidated. It consisted of two small bedrooms, a lounge room large enough to accommodate one four-seater couch, a tiny kitchen and a bath that took over an hour to fill to a level where you could soak more than just the bare essentials.

Despite all this, we loved living at the farm. Before long it became the unofficial doss house for anyone who needed a day or two on the couch. More often than not, the days became weeks. In fact, I can't remember a time in our two years at the farm when the four official tenants were the only residents.

Very early in the piece at Eltham, I invited my mate Danny Harkin to come over from Broadmeadows with some young people he was working with at the CYSS project there. Danny was (and is) a larger-than-life character. For the past four years, he had been working with one of the most notorious gangs in Broadmeadows, the 'J.A. Sharps'. This was quite funny because Danny would have easily got a job as an extra on the set of *Easy Rider*, with his almost waist-long hair, Ned Kelly-style beard and black 650cc Yamaha, which had been customised to fit the 'rat bike from hell' image.

For some reason that still eludes me, Danny and I had acquired a small fleet of Commer vans in various stages of disrepair. If we'd cannibalised all of them, we would have been lucky to get one to a roadworthy state. That included the one Danny was driving.

As part of our continued effort to have West meet East, Danny brought two or three guys across to the farm to teach us all the finer points of welding. Unlike me, Danny had completed his apprenticeship as a motor mechanic and had worked in the industry for a short time before becoming a youth worker. What better way to teach new skills than by experience? So we decided to cut up one of the Commers for practice. It was great fun. Everyone was learning the intricacies of oxyacetylene use, and within a couple of hours all that was left of the Commer was the rolling chassis, the windscreen and the steering wheel.

Now, I didn't want to add to the junkyard appearance of our pristine ten acres any more than necessary. It was bad enough as it was. We had inherited three or four dead Kombi vans when we moved in. Add the Commers, my beautiful FJ Holden, the occasional FC Holden, a couple of horse floats, some dead farm machinery and a few motorbikes, and I reckoned ten acres was only just going to be enough. So we decided to take the remains of the welding project to the tip, using one of the other Commers as the tow vehicle.

I drove the tow vehicle with my orange mane flying in the breeze, while Danny stood at the steering wheel of the rolling chassis, wearing his leather jacket and leather flying helmet, complete with split-lens goggles, lambswool scarf and a pose that would have done Donald Sutherland proud in *THE DIRTY DOZEN*. Looking through the cracked rear-view mirror, I could hardly see for the tears in my eyes. We certainly managed to turn a few heads. Two of the heads we managed to turn were in a police car that was heading in the opposite direction. In fact, as we passed each other, the coppers' heads turned so fast I thought they were going to have whiplash. Nervously I watched them pull over, then continue on in their original direction. Phew! That was close.

When I got into work the next day, there was a message for me. The local police sergeant wanted to have a word with me, and my boss's boss wanted a word with me afterwards. The motor mechanic and welding programs took a lower profile in the ensuing months, and no, I hadn't considered how as an employee of the Shire of Eltham my professional conduct would impact on the impeccable reputation of the Shire. Welcome to Eltham.

One of the main reasons I was employed at Eltham was to improve the participation of young people in both the CYSS project and the shire-owned drop-in centre. The CYSS project was located in a former doctor's surgery in Luck Street called Yootha House. No-one knew why it was called Yootha House, and no-one felt the need to change the name.

When I first started at Yootha House, it had all the energy of a viewing parlour at an undertaker's. The first thing I did was procure a ghetto blaster and fill the place up with a bit of music. A very small handful of daily regulars would turn up at 9 a.m., usually because their anxious parents had kicked them out of the house in the vain hope they would look for work. There was plenty of looking, but always to no avail.

The young people who patronised Yootha House all had significant personal and interpersonal problems. Sadly, it was unlikely that many of them would ever be employed, though they were all magnificent human beings and deserved our support. The problem was that their presence made it virtually impossible to attract new participants. Other kids would venture in, take one look and not come back, unless they identified with those already there.

The problem of servicing the needs of the growing numbers of unemployed young people was compounded by the fact that no-one wanted to use the Shire's drop-in centre, a huge old factory in the middle of town. Instead, the local 'hooligans' would hang around in the shopping arcade, intimidating the ratepayers. It became my job to make contact with this 'rowdy' crowd and see what I could do to get them out of the arcade and into the drop-in centre.

I was acutely aware that I was being used as an agent of social control, so I suggested I first make contact with the group to find out what they wanted and how they felt about using the drop-in centre. I did this partly out of respect for the young people and partly because I knew that if they didn't want to use the centre for whatever reason, then it was unlikely anything I would say would change their minds, and I would be seen to have 'failed'.

As it turned out, making contact was easy. I just hung around the only Space Invader machine in Eltham, marvelling at the skills of some of the players and asking the occasional question about the finer points of the game. Given my Afro, beard and feral jumper, it wasn't hard to build rapport. It felt a bit like being undercover, except I wasn't there to bust anybody. I was there to gain their confidence and their trust.

After stacking bricks, I couldn't believe I was getting paid to do what I was doing. For a month or so my day consisted of getting up around 10 a.m., heading down to Woolies arcade around 11 or 12, and playing or watching Space Invaders for a few hours while building relationships with my new mates. They all knew I worked for the Shire, but they didn't seem to mind.

After a few weeks I asked a couple of the more popular guys how they would feel if I could get hold of the Council minibus and go to the night football at VFL Park.

'D'ja reckon you could get it?' they asked incredulously.

'I reckon I could, if we could guarantee nobody would trash it or throw up in it,' I replied.

The deal was struck. I left it to them to figure out which twelve were to fill the limited number of seats, and we arranged to meet at my office at the drop-in centre at 6.30 p.m., a good half an hour earlier than necessary.

The chosen twelve arrived on the dot of 6.30 p.m., and I invited them inside to wait, as I had a few things I had to do before we left. Soon they were all playing table tennis and pool, much to my boss's delight. It wasn't long before the drop-in centre became the regular home base for the 25 or 30 kids who had previously been hanging around the shopping arcade. My strategy had worked, largely because the young people had been given a choice. I also made sure they were invited to plan and develop the activities we conducted.

Once the drop-in centre was fulfilling its potential, I had a solid base from which to work. I was now able to be of far greater value to the young people, many of whom had significant and complex needs – no income support, drug dependencies, outstanding criminal charges, insecure accommodation and so on. Yootha House continued to offer a place to go and social contact for the small group with high support needs who literally had nowhere else to turn to for support, assistance or a place in the community.

For some time now I had been convinced that the situation facing many young people was absolutely unacceptable and completely unnecessary. I couldn't understand why so many young people were treating each other appallingly, with gang violence and so on, and why governments of all persuasions could not seem to get it right when dealing with them. It was obvious to me that the more pressure you put on people, the worse they would behave. I had witnessed some disgraceful behaviour, yet I knew those concerned, and in the main they were fundamentally good people.

At this stage, I was just starting to realise how important it is to distinguish between people and their behaviour. There is a world of difference between condemning people as individuals and telling them that their behaviour is unacceptable. This would later become a significant operating principle in my work with young people. This is not to say that people are not responsible for their behaviour, but it is extremely important to make the distinction. By doing this, I was able to recognise the true brilliance in every young person I met. I have often been heard saying to a young person, 'You are a magnificent human being, but this behaviour sucks.' I believe it is really important to challenge unacceptable behaviour, but it is equally important to do so in a way that doesn't make the individual wrong.

With the wisdom of hindsight, I think the model adopted for the Community Youth Support Scheme (CYSS) was quite a good one, in that the federal government gave money directly to local groups to create and deliver local solutions to support young people in their community. In reality, though, the scheme was largely a disaster. Most groups did not have a clue about how to support young people effectively, and the projects became drop-in centres for those who were most isolated. Positive, solution-focused groups were hard if not impossible to find.

While I was grateful for the opportunity to get into youth work, I felt we were doing little more than providing a baby-sitting service for a very small number of young people. I was convinced we had to be able to do better than this. I had gained valuable experience at Eltham under the mentorship of my boss and friend Jan Loughman. At the same time, Jane and I had been experiencing how the other half lived out with the hippies in Eltham, not realising yet there were many more 'other halves' out there in the big wide world. After eighteen months or so, I was restless and dissatisfied again. I began looking for a new job.

The job I took was as an outreach youth worker with the young people of the Carlton high-rise housing estate. Carlton is an inner-city suburb with a strong working-class history. From the 1960s onwards, the middle class had moved in, gentrified the area and made it harder for lower-income people to remain. Slap bang in the middle of Carlton, however, were the high-rise public housing estates. From memory, at the time there were more than 10,000 people living literally on top of each other in less than a square kilometre, with virtually no support services or social infrastructure. This was a larger population than most country towns, which had their own schools, health services and hospitals (or they did in the 1970s), golf clubs, service clubs, sports clubs and facilities and so on. While a lot of people were proud to live in the high rise, the estates were a social disaster.

Fortunately I was employed by the Church of All Nations – affectionately known as 'CAN' – which had a great reputation in the high rise. This made establishing rapport and credibility much easier. CAN is located in the shadows of the high rise, and was the main source of welfare support for the people of the estate. I got to meet some excellent people – mums, kids, the occasional dad, not to mention being on first-name terms with the police senior sergeant and the local magistrate.

Life in the high rise was pretty raw. There were large numbers of single mums with two or three kids, large numbers of kids who would often run in packs, and most of the men I met were terminally unemployed or on pensions. It was the kids who ran the place. Most of the mums were 'upstairs', alone and isolated, while the kids were in strong peer groups and out of control. My role was largely to work with the kids, to give them someone to talk to or support them if they needed it.

Gangs were a feature of life in the estate, but by and large the only serious trouble was between 'the Carlton Boys' and gangs from other areas. From what I could gather, despite their well-deserved ferocious reputation, the 'Carlton Boys' consisted of no more than fifteen or twenty young men, mostly aged from seventeen to their early twenties. The gang had its share of angry young men, and the occasional interesting character as well.

One time, not long after I had started working in Carlton, a few of the mums asked if I would help to run a disco for the younger kids of the estate in the community hall under the main high-rise block. As happens with most events, the bulk of the workload fell to a few. One of the prime movers was a woman called Val, who was universally recognised as a leader in the high-rise community. Val was a great woman. She had a hard-as-nails exterior, but would do anything for most people. When people had a problem they couldn't resolve, they would often go to Val before going to see a social worker or counsellor.

She was a big woman in every sense of the word. Most people liked or admired her, but I believe they were also a bit scared of her. I know I was. Whenever I witnessed Val in action, usually with a teenager who was behaving unacceptably, I would thank God she was on my side.

Within a couple of weeks we had begged or borrowed the equipment and booked a DJ, who offered to do the job at a much-discounted rate. It was the only way we could get anything done. Disposable income was not a big feature in this environment, and getting a couple of hundred dollars from the Melbourne City Council or the Ministry for Housing was like trying to strike a wet match on a plate of jelly: plenty of activity without much result.

It was a balmy Saturday night in November. Daylight saving had not long been in. Daylight saving and warm weather usually meant a larger than usual gathering of people downstairs, sitting around the common grassed areas, and an increase in beer consumption. The publican of the Woolpack Hotel, which backed on to the high-rise estate, used to run a very reliable line of credit between Welfare Wednesdays, which came each fortnight. So, despite not having much cash, people could always be sure of a slab while their credit rating was good.

We didn't need to market the disco very much, other than to let people know it was for kids under sixteen. The rest would be at the pubs and clubs anyhow, and under no circumstance was anyone to bring grog or turn up under the influence of drugs. Illicit drugs were not a huge problem back then – unlike alcohol, which was as much a part of life as football, meat pies, kangaroos and Holden cars.

The disco got off to a fine start. Three or four mums and myself represented the security. Once the kids were inside, there wasn't much for us to do. Though they numbered in their hundreds, they were all exceptionally well behaved. Then, around 10.30 p.m., a young kid came bolting in, almost taking the double-glazed glass door off its hinges and screaming blue murder. He ran straight to Val and told her that a rival gang from Brunswick was heading this way in search of the Carlton Boys.

Without flinching, Val sent one of the young boys upstairs to let her partner and his mates know what was happening. This was important, because the hall we were in only had one doorway, so if someone blocked the exit we would all be trapped. Adrenalin was pumping as a mixture of fear and excitement filled the room.

When Val told me what was about to happen, I said I would go to the front door and do my best to prevent the approaching gang from entering the hall.

'You're a gutsy little bastard, aren't ya?' she replied. As I walked towards the door, I heard Val complete her compliment: 'No fucking brains. Gutsy, but.'

I walked outside and told the person behind me to lock the doors. I took about five steps towards where I believed the gang to be approaching. Then I saw them. Holy shit! I don't know what I was expecting, but I assure you it wasn't what I saw. Without exaggeration, there were fifty or sixty young men heading in my direction, all carrying weapons. Their approach was alarmingly stealthy. If the Carlton Boys had been there, it would have been a bloodbath.

Remembering my days at the Craigieburn shops, I began a dialogue to defuse a potential disaster. Unfortunately, calling in the cavalry was out of the question. This was before the era of mobile phones, and the Ministry for Housing, true to form, hadn't provided a phone in the hall.

'What can I do for you, boys?' I asked.

'Where are the Carlton Boys?'

'They're not here.'

'Bullshit! They're in that hall. Let me see.'

'Sorry, mate, I can't let you guys in there. It's a private function for little kids, and if I let you in I'll lose my job. I tell you what - one of you can come with me to have a look. Other than a couple of women and a bunch of 13-year-olds, there isn't anyone else in the place. The Carlton Boys are in Brunswick somewhere looking for someone.' (I knew that would wind them up.) 'So if you want a quick squiz I will let one of you in - unarmed, of course.'

Why they didn't just move me to one side and keep going is still a mystery to me, but they didn't. The ringleader was naturally suspicious. He thought that if the Carlton Boys were inside and he went in, they would have him trapped.

It was a very tense moment. He said something to his gang in Turkish and gestured with his head for a 'volunteer' to go with me. An even more nervous young boy stepped forward, handed his two-foot piece of galvanised pipe to the leader, and tentatively followed me to the door of the hall. The door opened just wide enough to allow us both to enter.

The young scout scanned the room in record time. Before long he was outside and apparently feeling more confident.

'Did you look in the toilets?' the leader asked.

'Yes,' he lied.

'I told you, they are in Brunswick somewhere,' I chipped in, anxious to move them on.

Just as they were turning – to head for Brunswick, I assume – Val opened the hall door and began a torrent of abuse.

'G'worn, fuck off, ya dagoes!'

I couldn't believe it. I thought I was a dead man. But from the windows of the hall she'd seen something I hadn't. Her bloke and about a dozen of his mates from the Woolpack were approaching. They too began yelling abuse. On closer inspection I saw that every single one of them was brandishing a pistol, sawn-off shotgun, or in one case a semi-automatic rifle.

'Go on, fuck off!' was the order of the day. And wisely, they did.

My heart was thumping as if I had just completed a marathon. Val appeared from the hall and began abusing her bloke. 'Where the fuck have you been, ya hopeless bastard? Ya left it up to the little bloke! You're as weak as piss!' And on she went. I had never heard anyone abuse someone armed with a pistol the way Val abused this poor bugger. Then she turned to the rest of the men – all armed to the back teeth – and they all stood there like Grade 6 children being admonished by the principal.

Eventually, Val's bloke turned to me and said, 'Sorry, mate. We were gunna come over a bit earlier but we sorta got stuck in the pub. Yer know 'ow it is sometimes? I'll tell ya what, come back to the pub with us, an' we'll shout ya a couple fer ya effort.'

Though I was in desperate need of a drink and recognised the honour being bestowed, I passed on the offer. I said I'd definitely drop in and take them up on it at a later date.

Val's bloke turned to me and said, 'Fair enough, mate. Here, look after me shooter in case those pricks come back' – handing me his pistol.

'Nah, it's OK, mate. I'd probably end up shooting myself,' I replied, only half jokingly.

'Fair enough,' he said, and with that the men departed. I had just had my first encounter with the Melbourne underworld.

*

When I was working at the high rise, I didn't have a clue what I was doing or meant to be doing. I think I was like many youth workers of the day, good **WITH** young people, but not necessarily good **FOR** them. It was still early days in the development of the professional youth work industry. The popular theory was that you should act as an advocate for your client, but looking around the place it didn't seem to be making much difference.

I was caught up in a not-always-subtle game

of cops and robbers. The kids would largely do what they wanted to. The cops would chase them and often charge them, whether they thought they were guilty or not. The cops' logic seemed to be that if they didn't do it they knew who did – and besides, this is for the stuff we know you did that we didn't catch you doing. The cops would charge the kid, the kid would come to me pleading innocence, I would arrange a 'mouthpiece' via the Legal Aid system (yes, we had one then), and we would all front up to the Magistrate's or Children's Court. The kid would invariably plead not guilty unless the mouthpiece had struck a deal out the front. The magistrate would find him guilty, then the mouthpiece would put me in the stand, where I would tell the court what a great kid he was and how a custodial sentence would be a detrimental event in his life. Usually I would have organised a better option than a jail sentence and more often than not the magistrate would take the alternative option.

I did this three or four times a week. It was a vicious circle, and again I was left thinking that surely we as a society could come up with something better than this crazy way to live. Isolated mums, absent fathers, out-of-control kids, frustrated coppers, overworked courts, wealthy lawyers. Actually, that's not fair. The only lawyers who would take the kids on were those who were committed to the Community Legal Services – either that, or they couldn't get a job elsewhere.

I was working twelve-hour days and gradually becoming worn out by the futility of it all. I was beginning to doubt that there was anything one person could do. It was getting all too hard. Apart from staying off the dole queue, there was little point remaining in youth work. The problems appeared too great and the resources too small.

I was still relatively young, and I was yet to realise that where you put your attention and focus, you will expand. All of my focus was on the problems, so guess what continued to expand? This was draining my energy, so once again I decided to move on.

Jane's parents had moved to the Gippsland Lakes in the east of Victoria, some 300 kilometres from Melbourne. The region was idyllic, with the largest inland lake system in Australia and the Ninety Mile Beach, which lives up to its name. Bairnsdale, the regional centre, had about the same population as the high-rise estate I had left behind.

An old mate, Myke Ziolo, had already moved into the area and was involved in community education. Myke was the guy who had offered me the job at St Albans, so it was great to work with him at last. I was employed to create and manage an Education Program for Unemployed Youth. This was another national labour market program, and this time the emphasis was on preparing the long-term unemployed for work by using a more structured, classroom-based approach.

Me in the classroom again – well, that was a turn-up! Fortunately Myke had also employed a couple of very good ex-teachers, so with our collective experience we were able to put together a twenty-week program that to our credit the young people continued to attend.

I was pretty hopeless in the classroom. My

emerging talent was building networks and contacts in the broader community, including employers. Almost all of the young people who gained employment through that program did so as a result of our networking with employers, including the local municipalities.

I learnt a great deal from Myke Ziolo. Myke was a brilliant communicator, very charming, enthusiastic and with loads of energy. He was amazingly persuasive and great influencer of people, regardless of their station or lack of it. We got on well. We helped create a Regional Economic Development Board, one of the first in Victoria, as well as a Regional Network of Technical and Further Education for the socially and geographically isolated people of Far East Gippsland.

By now I was beginning to find my feet as a professional community worker. I had completed a tertiary qualification in community work by studying part-time over a number of years. I was beginning to get a sense that we might start to get somewhere if we could get a broad section of the community together to co-operate in creating local employment solutions, while at the same time skilling up young people so that when they got a job they knew how to keep it. I was keen, enthusiastic, energetic and incredibly optimistic. I am afraid my optimism always far outweighed my patience. Before long, I was becoming frustrated and disillusioned.

I eventually blew my stack at a meeting of the Regional Economic Development Board. After what seemed like an eternity, a conversation about job creation was about to take another lap around the same loop when I suggested we begin by creating twenty job opportunities for the students in my program.

That was considered far too ambitious. People suggested that we should begin with one or two jobs as a starting point.

I couldn't believe it. In the room sat virtually all the movers and shakers in the region. There were representatives from three municipalities, local heads of three or four government departments, representatives of the chambers of manufacturing and commerce – the list went on. I am afraid I was less than diplomatic. I launched into a tirade about how bloody useless we all were. What was point of our existence if we couldn't manage to create a pathetic twenty jobs?

'I mean, what is the *POINT?*' I finished my tantrum by saying, 'We might all as well be pissing into the wind!'

Myke thought this was hilarious. When he left the region some time later, he reminded me of my infamous quote in his departure speech, with a brilliantly crafted poem delivered before the Who's Who of East Gippsland.

Throughout this time I was on the Youth Policy Development Council, which provided policy advice to the Victorian Minister for Youth Affairs and later the Premier. I was also involved in the Youth Affairs Council of Victoria, a peak body that was supposed to lobby governments on behalf of young people and youth services. Yet the more I got involved, the more frustrated I became. Tolerance and acceptance were not my strong suits – in fact, they are qualities I am still working to develop.

I had committed my admittedly brief adult life to trying to change how we as a society were treating our young people. So far, I had had very little success. I was tired, fed up and bored with my life. Jane and I decided to go our separate ways, despite our deep and significant relationship. I remember her once saying she had fulfilled her role in my life and now it was time to do something else. I will always be thankful for my ten great years of growing up with Jane, and we remain great mates.

So that was it. I was off. On the Gippsland Lakes, under the tutelage of Jane's father, Bob, I had developed a keen interest in sailing. Bob was a shipwright and wooden boat enthusiast of the old school. He was a wiry little Glaswegian who did his apprenticeship on the Clyde River during the halcyon days of Scottish boat-building. He used to say, 'If God wanted us to make fibreglass boats, he would have made fibreglass trees.'

I decided to check this sailing caper out properly, and booked a one-way ticket to London. I was going to sail the seven seas.

3
In Search of Self

Travelling alone was a treat. I wanted to go by myself partly to discover more of who I was. I had always suspected I was a fairly resourceful person, but I didn't really know for sure. I had gone from living with my parents to living with Jane, and I had never really done anything on my own before. After a brief 'Aussie abroad' experience in London, I made my way to Manchester to stay with two cousins who had grown up in Craigieburn before their parents decided to return home after ten years in Australia. I soon found myself working in a specialist tennis store. Pat Cash had just won Wimbledon and I was Australian, so it stood to reason I knew everything there was to know about tennis, right?

One day, the owner had gone out and I was on my own in the shop when a sales rep turned up with 150 oversize tennis racquets, which had retailed the previous season for £150 each. He said we could have them for £30 each if I took ten or more. I said we would take all of them if he made the price £20. 'Done!' was the firm reply.

'Great,' I said. 'Leave 50 of them and we will pay you on consignment.'

Oversize racquets have limited appeal. They look like snowshoes, and are never going to be a fashion item. Their main value is that they make it easier for elderly players or young kids to hit the ball. I went through the Yellow Pages contacting senior citizens groups, a couple of tennis clubs and two private schools. Before the owner came back, I had generated orders for 75 of them at £60 each, less than half price! By the end of the week I was ringing the rep and wanting to order more, but unfortunately the line had been discontinued. The owner of the shop gave me half the profit as a bonus and vowed not to leave me alone in the shop again.

It was around this time that I saw an ad in one of the British national newspapers. 'Wanted: crew to deliver yachts – South France-Greece.' You beauty, I thought. I called the number and it was an Australian who answered the phone.

'Where you from?'

'Melbourne – well, actually, East Gippsland. I sailed in the lakes.'

'Whereabouts in East Gippsland?'

I told the guy I had lived in a few places. When he said 'I'm from Lindenow South', I nearly fell over. Lindenow South is a tiny village near Bairnsdale with a population of about 100 people. It turned out I had played football against this guy and we had quite a few mutual friends. Needless to say, I got the job.

The sailing was terrific. I was one of about 40 crew delivering a fleet of new 30-foot yachts from Juan le Pair to Greece. It was like a progressive party from harbour to harbour. Once I was introduced into the subculture of the sailing world, getting the next sail was easy.

Then a woman I met on one of the deliveries

invited me to stay in Ipswich, England. Her name was Maggie; she was a feisty little Scot and very handy on the foredeck. Part of the reason she invited me was so I could help crew in the cross-Channel races she took part in most weekends.

While I was in Ipswich I heard about a job going at Suffolk College, the region's largest tertiary institute, for a lecturer in sociology. No worries, I thought; I'm sociable. After two intensive interviews and an assurance that I would send home for my qualifications, I got the job. It was a piece of cake too. Once again I found it hard to believe I was getting well paid for this. Start at 9 a.m., finish at 3.30 p.m., and an hour for lunch.

I was settling in very nicely when the Dean of the faculty asked me in for a 'chat'. Bugger, I thought. It must be about my qualifications, which not surprisingly had failed to arrive. Wrong. The Dean told me he was very impressed with the way I had fitted into life at the college and the staff thought I was quite an asset to the faculty. He offered me a 12-month extension on my contract with the option of joining the permanent staff after that.

Bloody hell. I was in a real quandary. I was really enjoying the job, which, as I saw it, was basically about inviting the students to think for themselves – a concept that had never been tried before. The terms and conditions were the best I had ever experienced in my life, the sailing on the weekend was great. But . . . that night on TV there was a documentary about the ARC, a sailing rally across the Atlantic Ocean from Las Palmas in the Canary Islands to Barbados. Straight away I knew. I hadn't come over here to be a teacher; I came to sail, to check life out and to explore the planet.

The next morning I went to see the Dean and told him that I was grateful but I would be declining his offer, because I was off to sail across the Atlantic. I remember him smiling through his teeth and muttering something about 'never understanding Orstraylians'. Most of the staff I told about my decision thought it was hilarious, apart from the couple who had been on three-month contracts for more than three years and were desperate to be offered permanency.

The next weekend I took off to London and made my way to St Catherine's Dock, the hub of sailing activity in London. I walked straight into the most prestigious sailing club in England, signed myself in under the last member on the register and bought myself a beer.

On the noticeboard was an ad for two crew members to sail a 27-foot Vancouver from Gibraltar to Las Palmas, then participate in the ARC. I looked at the ad again: 27 feet is not a lot of boat. I asked a couple of people if they knew the skipper, and they told me the ad had been there for a while. Apparently the size of the boat had put a lot of people off. Funny, that.

I rang the owner and arranged a meeting for the next week. I said that I would be in it if I could talk a mate of mine into filling the other berth. My logic was simple: if I could bring along my sailing mate Graham, an Australian bloke I had met on one of the yacht deliveries, I could be sure at least one of the three of us knew how to sail well.

The trip from Gibraltar to Las Palmas was horrible. Instead of taking six days it took nine.

For three days and two very long nights we were hove to, going up and down on the spot in horrendously big seas. It was all we could do to avoid going backwards, as there was a gale-force wind right on our nose. The one positive was knowing that if the little boat could survive this, crossing the Atlantic where all the conditions are favourable would be a doddle. We were right.

The preparation for the crossing was an outstanding event. Over 200 vessels attending to last-minute details. All of the participating boats were moored in purpose-built pens in the harbour. There was a great camaraderie and sense of community. In two weeks we would all be heading south for a few days before wheeling ourselves around to the west, destination Barbados!

One old bloke I met in a bar suggested that crossing the Atlantic these days with all the new gizmos like satellite navigation was no big deal. 'Not like the ol' days,' he went on. 'In the ol' days you headed south, and when the butter melted, you turned right. That's how you got to Barbados.'

At this time, quite by accident, I began to discover some more of my entrepreneurial qualities. One balmy evening when the temperature was its predictable 28 degrees, I decided to invite the other yachties in our pen to a barbecue. I 'borrowed' a 44-gallon drum and had it cut in half, one for the barbecue and the other for the ice. I collected the equivalent of $5.00 from everybody and went about organising some meat, beers and ice. Given my Spanish, it was an extraordinary achievement. We had enough to feed the five thousand. That reminds me, better get some bread!

The evening was a fabulous success, with people coming from far and wide. The aroma of barbecued chicken served as the dinner bell, and before long out came the guitars, and people I had never laid eyes on were wanting to know how much for a beer or some chicken. By the end of the night I was $100 better off and I had a request from another pen to organise a barbecue for them. 'Sure,' I said. 'You collect $10 from everyone and I will organise the food and drinks.'

This went on for two weeks, with different pens playing host for the party. It was virtually the same crowd every night, and it really brought people together – not to mention financing my sailing around the Caribbean for six months.

About two days before the start of the rally, I noticed a huge pile of blue T-shirts with the ARC motif on the front taking up space in the organisers' office. When I asked what they were doing there, I was told they represented a large disappointment to the organisers, who were sure they would have sold much better than they had. Not sitting in a corner, I thought.

They said I could have them for $2 each so they could recoup their costs. No worries. I loaded up a trolley and walked from pen to pen asking people if they had got their souvenir commemorative T-shirt yet and what size they were.

'Sorry, we've only got large left. Here ya go, that will be ten bucks, thanks.'

Within a day I had sold out and was telling people I would see what I could do about getting some more printed in Barbados. Sure beat the hell out of stacking bricks!

4
Back into it

I did pretty well on my travels, considering that when I left Australia I was little more use than live ballast. I had sailed around Britain, raced in cross-Channel races, sailed the Dutch canals, delivered yachts to Sicily, crossed the Atlantic and spent six months sailing around the Caribbean. Life was pretty good for this kid from Craigieburn who only ten years earlier had hardly heard of Blackburn!

Eventually, though, I realised my sailing time was up. One afternoon I was lying in the blunt end of the boat, and a friend asked where we were sailing to the next day. I couldn't remember. Martinique, I thought.

He kept asking questions. 'What's the date today? The day? What's the name of this harbour again?'

I made light of the conversation, but the truth was that I wasn't exactly sure of any of the answers. Then he said, 'Oh, well, I'll see you at happy hour', and although I wasn't wearing a watch I knew it was eight minutes away. It was definitely time to go home.

I had tested my mettle over the past couple of years. In many ways, I had begun the journey of getting to know myself and understanding some of my strengths and weaknesses. I had also gained a greater appreciation of my creative and entrepreneurial capabilities. I had left Australia with $4000, and after travelling for two years I arrived back with one English five-pound note.

It was time to go back to work. I wasn't sure what I was going to do when I got home. All I knew was that I wasn't going to get back into youth work. What a joke!

Soon I found casual work doing sleepover shifts at youth refuges. It wasn't much different from my days hanging around the streets of Broadmeadows. This was definitely 'not it'. Then one of my dearest mates, John Tripodi, told me there was a job going as co-ordinator of a youth service in Port Melbourne. If I got it, I would be his boss. We both thought this would be a bit of a giggle, so I went for the job and got it.

I had met John back in Bairnsdale, when he was the manager of a similar program in Sale, some 80 kilometres away. I will always remember the first time we met. It was at a softball match organised between the Bairnsdale and Sale EPUY programs. John bounded up enthusiastically, stuck his hand out and said 'G'day, I'm Troppo.'

I studied him carefully for a second or two and said, 'Yeah, I believe that.'

In true Troppo style, he was wearing a pair of purple and black checked pants, a bright green, red and yellow woollen jumper and a smile that I swear must have stretched his head.

'I do what you do in Sale, only better,' he added, and from that moment until his premature death aged 40, I was closer to John than to most other people on the planet.

When you are fortunate enough to come across a truly outstanding human being, you treasure the relationship. With John you won the lottery. Whenever he met anyone, no matter who they were, he was able to connect with them in a way that made them feel special. I know I did. Troppo was the only bloke I know that had a couple of hundred best friends. He was extraordinarily generous with his love and affection. Once John formed a friendship with anyone, that was it. It was for keeps.

He would often astound me by saying, 'Remember so and so?' – maybe someone we met years earlier at a conference – 'Well, I had lunch with them yesterday and they said to say g'day.'

We were like brothers. As brothers do sometimes, we fell out for a while, and that was OK; it was part of our journey together. My first couple of years back in Melbourne tested our friendship to breaking point.

South Port Youth Service, or SPYS as it was called, was auspiced and managed by Melbourne City Mission, which at the time was in expansion mode. I thought this was great. I was ambitious and saw big opportunities for the organisation and myself.

Before long I was the Regional Manager for the Inner Urban Region of Melbourne, which covered a range of services, including a youth refuge and an information service as well as SPYS. I was on a crusade to build my empire. We created several pilot programs that were considered to be at the leading edge, and we managed to attract significant philanthropic support. I learnt many important lessons during my time at Melbourne

City Mission, some of them at great expense, including to my relationship with all of my staff. I was out of control, hell-bent on making things happen.

As I have said, patience, tolerance and reasonableness are not my strong suits, and in this environment they were not particularly useful qualities. Although governments, philanthropists, and to a lesser degree business had spent millions of dollars trying to solve the problems facing many of our young people, every measurable indicator was heading in the wrong direction. Youth unemployment, homelessness, drug addiction, fatal overdoses and illicit drug use, crime, the number of kids incarcerated, suicide – need I go on? In this situation, patience, tolerance and reasonableness were not useful qualities at all. In fact, I still believe we all ought to be totally impatient, completely intolerant and absolutely bloody unreasonable in our pursuit of a community that treats all its people with respect, dignity, love, understanding and acceptance.

Regrettably, my impatience led to a major falling-out with John a couple of years after I began working at SPYS. In hindsight, part of the problem was that we were friends as well as work colleagues. I am sure that if either of us had been able to see or do things differently at the time we would have.

It was at a time when I was sick of the youth sector's culture of decision (or lack of it) by committee. In my opinion, people were so concerned with the process that they paid very little regard to any outcome. I didn't give a toss about the process – I just wanted a result! A bit of both was probably the answer, but as a result of this conflict John and I grew poles apart.

John was responsible for the development of a youth policy for the municipalities of South Melbourne and Port Melbourne. His position and the youth policy were funded entirely by Mayne Nickless through its Corporate Affairs Department. Obviously in order to develop a youth policy there needs to be a large amount of community consultation, but from where I sat pretty well all I saw were the same four or five youth workers turning up to two or three meetings a week for over eighteen months. As the boss, I felt I had to account to all the stakeholders: Mayne Nickless, the Melbourne City Mission, both municipalities and the community.

John became enormously frustrated with me, saying I wouldn't listen and I was trying to undermine him. Eventually he resigned to take up a new career with a company that sold and managed retirement villages. There was probably some truth in his first charge, but regardless of who was right and who was wrong, I know I was the poorer for his leaving.

One Saturday night, about eighteen months after John had resigned, the phone rang at about 11.30 p.m. It was John. He apologised for calling so late and told me he had to talk to me, now. He was in the middle of a personal development workshop called The Forum, where one of the processes was to get on the phone to someone with whom you had unfinished business.

We talked for more than four hours. We laughed, we cried, we told the truth as we saw it, and we heard each other from a position of love and respect. We vowed to rebuild our relationship, and we did from that night on.

*

Meanwhile, I had become engaged in a running battle with the bureaucracy that ran the state care system. It was clear to me that we had got it wrong in the area of 'state care' – an oxymoron if ever there was one. The state by definition cannot and does not care. At best, it may be able to protect young people from harm, but it cannot care. There were plenty of people working in state care who did care – the overwhelming majority, in fact – but the system itself was designed to fail.

When dealing with complex human beings – not to mention families – it is sometimes necessary to take well-judged risks, but the state care system was dominated by fear of making a mistake or being exposed for being careless. Bureaucrats feared anyone who had the courage to think creatively, speak up or question the results we were achieving. Their job was to administer the existing programs within the allocated budget and guidelines, with the minimum of fuss or disruption. Anything else represented a threat. The only people who survived for any length of time within the system were those who were patient, tolerant and reasonable. The rest either became burnt out or were spat out.

The system also made no distinction between kids who were in the system because they were deemed in need of 'care and protection' and those who were there because they had been convicted of committing crimes. Kids were treated like criminals for being born into families who were unable or unprepared to care for them. Many of the kids who entered the system for 'protection' ended up in the juvenile justice system after committing petty crimes, which were often futile attempts to make someone listen to their cries of frustration.

Many of these kids only wanted to be at home in a loving family. Yet, for whatever reason, incredibly, they were asking too much. The hurt, the pain of rejection and the resentment often came out in harmful and destructive behaviour – sniffing solvents, self-mutilation, prostitution or violence. This behaviour was very hard to be around, but it was even harder to resolve the issues that were the source of their personal turmoil.

In Victoria, deinstitutionalisation was in full swing. Recognising that large institutions, including orphanages and 'Children's Homes', had failed to meet the human needs of those unfortunate enough to land up in them, the government was closing institutions across the board. As part of that plan, the government set up new 'care' facilities known as Early Adolescent Units or EAUs. From the outside, to all intents and purposes they looked like average family homes in the suburbs. The major difference was that there was no family: the young teenage residents were there by order of the courts, and were supervised by child-care workers, many of whom were unqualified, untrained and inexperienced.

I had the unenviable task of overseeing the supervisor of an EAU in Middle Park, and was ultimately responsible for the management of its $250,000 annual budget. This was a classic example of designing something to fail. The EAU provided medium to long-term accommodation for young people aged between eleven and sixteen. Not one of these young people wanted to be there, so they were generally hostile. The workers who cared for them were paid less than anyone else in the youth sector, and at best they had completed a two-year certificate course in child care. Without exception, they were good people doing their very best in an extremely difficult environment.

The kids' behaviour was often outrageous. Usually the kids placed in EAUs were there because they were deemed to be 'uncontrollable' at home. In fact, if they weren't uncontrollable when they came in, they sure as hell were by the time they got out.

They only went to school if they felt like it or to meet their friends – not that the schools complained, because the teachers' lives were much more peaceful when the kids stayed away. It wasn't unusual to see one of these kids hop on the back of the light rail and tram-surf to Fitzroy Street in St Kilda, where they could get stoned out of their pain and then turn a few tricks in one of the infamous street prostitution strips for more cash or more drugs. Some of these kids, boys and girls, were only twelve or thirteen years old. Although we had the full force of the law and the state behind us, we were powerless to do anything other than lock them up 'for their own good'. The situation facing more and more of our kids was getting worse, not better. It was, and still is, a bloody outrage.

In my eyes, the EAUs left a great deal to be desired. The kids would have been better off at home than receiving the 'care' we were providing on behalf of the state. But this was not what the Department of Community Services of Victoria wanted to hear – nor anyone else for that matter, barring a couple of other agitators like myself.

The Department could not allow the kids to go home, because it has a legislative responsibility to ensure the safety of those made state wards by the courts. (The Minister is the legal guardian of all the wards of the state.) I argued that we would all be better off if we gave the kids' families even half the money it cost each year to house a kid in an EAU. This was heresy, I know, but honestly these kids were every bit as much at risk of harm and moral danger in 'state care' as anywhere else, and it was costing $52,000 per year per child in 1990 dollars. A thousand bucks a week, and we couldn't even get them to go to school, let alone begin to address their pain and hurt or do anything about the futile situation many of them faced.

The staff turnover at the EAU was so rapid that I considered putting a turnstile on the gate, and the few staff who remained were stressed out of their brains and frequently on sick leave. Surely we could do better than this? I know it is easy to blame the government or the bureaucracy. They are easy targets, and often they do not do much to help themselves. It was only later that I realised the bureaucracy is there to manage the past, not design the future. Silly bugger me. No wonder I was frustrated, and in turn I became the source of much frustration to others.

Along with a few like-minded youth workers, I suggested that the department expand the foster-care system. Children under the age of twelve could be cared for in the community by families who had been screened and specially trained to provide a home environment. Why not do the same for adolescents and use a fraction of the money spent on EAUs to do it? If you paid the foster families a decent amount for out-of-pocket expenses, everybody would be better off, and there would be financial savings for the taxpayer as well.

In the department, our ideas ran into a brick wall. You would have thought we were calling for compulsory castration for all state government employees (at least those eligible, which by no coincidence were those in decision-making positions). For twelve months we went around and around in circles, at the same time facing crisis after crisis at the EAUs. Stuff it, I thought. Let's do it ourselves.

With some excellent support from our organisation's fund-raising professionals, we were able to secure philanthropic funds for a three-year pilot program to recruit, train and support people from the community to be care providers in our Community Adolescent Placement Scheme, or CAPS, as it was called. (Everything had to have an acronym.) We reimbursed each care provider $150 per week, which was about what it cost to have a teenager in your home.

We needed someone to launch the scheme, so I contacted Brian Burdekin, the Human Rights Commissioner. He had just completed a national report highlighting the situation facing growing numbers of children and young people in

Australia, which he argued was worse than that in developing nations. He'd been quoted as saying, 'There are some things governments do not do very well. Taking care of young people is one of them' – or something along those lines. When I heard this, I thought, Mr Burdekin, you are my man.

To my delight and surprise, he accepted my invitation to launch the project. Having the Human Rights Commissioner present, and the publicity that came with him, also helped to ensure that the Department of Community Services graciously accepted their invitation to participate in the project. I didn't get a Christmas card from them that year, but in spite of a few minor hiccups the pilot succeeded and was expanded nationally. Now a young person who for whatever reason cannot safely live at home can theoretically live with a neighbour, supported and supervised by the state. It's not asking a lot, really.

Governments of all political persuasions have had a crack at solving 'the youth problem'. Unfortunately for young people, one of the effects of this is that they are seen as being 'a problem', individually and collectively. This upsets a lot of young people, and fair enough too. I am absolutely convinced we cannot solve the challenges we as a society face by government interventions and programs alone. A programmatic approach cannot resolve human pain and suffering, isolation, fears and alienation. Human beings need human beings who love them, care for them and protect them, and when necessary challenge them to be better than they think they can be. In short, we need each other.

There is a role for governments, of course. It is vital to get the big-ticket items right, like financing an accessible, affordable education system that provides the basis for young people to learn, grow and develop as educated citizens. But after a few years at SPYS I was becoming convinced that governments and their agents had a limited ability to meet our common human needs. I think we have to ask ourselves, 'What sort of society do I want to live in, or to raise children in?' I have yet to hear of a kid with a strong sense of self-worth who has killed himself deliberately. Sure, like all of us, some make mistakes, with tragic consequences. But if we all looked at our own families, streets, towns or cities and asked ourselves, 'What am I doing today to increase the levels of esteem, respect, confidence and contribution of every kid in my sphere of influence?', then the chances are we wouldn't need the state to intervene in the lives of so many of our young people.

There is little point blaming anyone or justifying the situation or denying that a problem exists by manipulating statistics. If we want things to change for the better, then it is up to each and every one of us to do something constructive, even if that means being unreasonable sometimes. And if at first you don't succeed . . . do something different.

Unfortunately back in 1990 I was less gracious, and I continued blaming the government. I was becoming increasingly frustrated at the lack of energy for facilitating positive change. 'What is wrong with people?' I would ask. Bloody government, what would they know? Bloody bureaucrats, impeding the future. Bloody this, bloody that. I had also become more autocratic as time went by, and was unpopular with my staff and in parts of the youth work sector. I wasn't a happy chap. As I later realised, I was looking in exactly 180 degrees in the wrong direction for the answers. I was looking outside.

In the midst of all this, I had reacquainted myself with an old friend, Sharon Kosmina. Sharon and I had been friends for more than ten years and I had always fancied her somewhat – but, as she put it, 'You were married to someone else, Paul.' Sharon had split up from a long-term relationship about the time Jane and I separated. She had spent the past couple of years soul-searching and re-establishing herself, as one does after a major break-up.

We fell deeply in love. Sharon was always my ideal of a magnificent woman. Gorgeous, smart, ambitious yet balanced, compassionate, beautiful and . . . she loved me. Everyone is entitled to one flaw. Throughout my tumultuous time at the Melbourne City Mission, my relationship with Sharon was one of the very few stable factors in my life.

Yet I was deeply unhappy. I felt trapped in my work, but I didn't believe I was qualified to do much else. I had now been working with youth services for twelve years or more. I knew pretty well what was happening in professional youth service delivery across the country, and it wasn't looking good. Millions of dollars were being spent and thousands of people were working in the industry, most of them good people doing their very best, but the situation facing young people was getting worse. I thought if any other industry was getting the results we were getting, you would close it down. It wasn't a position that was popular with my peers.

I was on the point of giving up – which is not part of my natural make-up, believe me – when a good friend told me she was enrolled in a personal development weekend, which began on the next Thursday and ran until late Sunday night. I had never heard of personal development courses before. The workshop cost $750, and she said, 'Why don't you consider doing it with me?' I could think of 750 reasons right away, but I had great respect for my friend's judgement, so I decided to check it out.

The course was called Money and You. Strange name for a workshop, I thought. I might go to half of it, because I had no money.

I went to the promoters' office and got talking to Stan Jordan, the co-owner of the business. After he'd outlined what the workshop was like, I said, 'It sounds interesting, but I don't have $750. I work with kids in welfare.' It was true that I didn't have a spare $750 at the time, but even if I had I would not have invested it in my education, and certainly not in the workshop.

Stan said, 'Fair enough. You can do it for free. There are more important things than money sometimes.' If you have plenty, I thought. I was taken aback by this stranger's generosity. I reluctantly thanked him and enrolled in the workshop, wondering what the hell I had gotten myself in for.

So there I was in a workshop with another 149 sceptical punters. I was very suspicious. I had no idea what was going on. The beaming faces of the support staff reminded me of the Christians.

The main difference was that this crowd were dressed immaculately. As you walked into the huge room where the workshop was held, there were rows and rows and rows of tables, all with white tablecloths neatly pinned to hold them in place. In front of each chair was a white four-ring binder with a packet of Textacolours in the front cover. We all managed to find a chair without looking at each other. Me, I wanted one in the back row nearest the exit. In the background was what at first sounded like piped music, which I later came to recognise as Pacobel's Canon in D.

The facilitator walked up the middle aisle to rapturous applause. Who the bloody hell is clapping, I thought. He hasn't said anything yet. Then he did. He was a Yank, and in that moment I thanked God that I hadn't spent $750 on this.

What I witnessed and experienced over the next few days was amazing, not that I was going to let on. In the workshop, there was a motto: 'In order for things to change, first I must.' The facilitator was extremely confronting, without necessarily being aggressive. He openly challenged some of our fundamental attitudes, beliefs and behaviours.

One of the first beliefs he challenged was that of personal responsibility. He wrote 'Responsibility' in large letters and drew a line under it where he wrote 'Lay Blame' and under that 'Justify'. He pointed out that the vast majority of people lived most of their lives 'below the line' in blame and justification. I looked around the room to see who on earth he could be meaning; other people were doing the same.

If your life isn't the way you want it to be, he said, then it is up to you to do something about it, as opposed to justifying why it isn't what you want or blaming someone else for your situation.

The workshop also introduced the concept of win-win situations. The premise was that, if we committed ourselves to helping each other to achieve what we wanted in life instead of competing and shafting each other, then we would all benefit. So why do people behave in a win-lose or lose-lose way? Largely because we have been brought up to think there isn't enough for everybody and to fear rather than embrace difference. Compound that with large egos, competitiveness and greed, and you have the recipe for the mess the planet is in.

He pointed out that huge numbers of people were dying each day of starvation or malnutrition-related disease, while in many other parts of the world farmers were being ordered to dump millions of tonnes of rice or destroy livestock for fear of flooding the market – for which read, reducing prices. If anyone put their hand up to argue why this might be the case or to suggest it wasn't their fault, he simply walked up and tapped the words 'Lay Blame' or 'Justify'.

'Look, it is really simple,' he would say. 'If you think it's OK for the equivalent of an average Aussie Rules football crowd to die each day while Australian farmers are shooting millions of sheep, then do nothing. If that is not OK with you, what are you going to do about it?' My first thought was that it would depend which team was playing, but I thought it indiscreet to say anything at this point.

He really stirred the possum. Each time someone attempted to rationalise the situation or distance themselves from it, he would simply tap the paper, raising the collective blood pressure to new heights each time.

Usually he would then call a fifteen-minute break, and in the next session we would be thrown into a high-energy game that more often than not was deliberately designed to illustrate win-lose behaviour. Most of the games required you to stake your own money, which brought the lessons home. It was very uncomfortable. I finished each game with more money than I started with. Until then, I hadn't realised how much of a win-lose player I was. The premise was that games are often a reflection of behaviour: how you play here is pretty much how you play life. For every 'winner' in the room there had to be a 'loser', and in the big picture we all lose by behaving in a win-lose manner.

This was all new ground for me. I began to realise that part of what was missing in the welfare industry was a willingness to ask the hard questions. People were too busy trying to survive and justify their organisations' existence while attempting to secure funding for the following year – not the most conducive environment for creativity.

I was relatively quiet for the first couple of days. The Yank with the microphone kept saying, 'You do not have to settle for less than an absolutely full and rich life. You can have anything you want. It's entirely up to you.' He said it once too often, and I decided I'd had enough. Before I had time to reconsider, I stuck my hand up and somebody put a roving mike in it.

'Listen,' I said, 'I have been listening to all this you-beaut stuff for a couple of days now, and it might be all right for you and people like this who have got 750 bucks to spend, but what about the people I work with? The kids I am committed to – the unemployed, the drug-affected, the homeless, the alienated – what about them?' Feeling pretty pleased with myself, I sat down.

In a broad Texan drawl he replied, 'Good question. What about them? And, more to the point, what are you going to do about it?'

I was back on my feet in a flash. 'Me, me? What am I going to do about it? Listen, buddy, let me tell you something. I've been working my arse off for years trying to do something about the crap that is going on out there. It's not my fault! I've been doing my bit!'

He shot back: 'And are you happy with your results? What about your own life–are you happy with that? Look, it is really simple. You can go on flapping your gums blaming everyone else and justifying your miserable results, but it ain't gonna make one iota of difference until you do something different. It is up to you. It is your life. The buck for your life stops with you. Your results, your life, you.'

For one of the first times in my life I was completely speechless. The screeching sounds inside my head were silenced. It was as if time had just been halted and I had entered another dimension.

He was right. The bloody Yank was right. I had spent so much of my life blaming others for what wasn't working, so long making excuses to justify my funding and my next year's wages, all the time thinking that I was behaving responsibly and trying to change the system. I felt perplexed.

I have no idea what happened for the rest of that day. I only know that my life was in turmoil with this simple yet profound realisation. What had I been doing for the past twelve years? Bloody hell. I was having an internal crisis. I felt the game I had been playing was up, and I did not know what to do. I couldn't go back to my familiar patterns of existence. That was over. I now realise that this was cause for celebration, but I was nowhere near being ready to see that.

I went home and Sharon was in bed.

'How was it?' she asked.

'I don't know,' I said, and I meant it.

My friend picked me up the next morning, and we returned for more of the same. About mid-morning the facilitator checked in with me to see how I was doing. 'I'm fine,' I lied. I spent the next part of the workshop paddling up that river in Egypt called denial. What problem? I haven't got a problem, just got a couple of things to sort out, that's all.

The truth was that I was deeply perturbed. The core beliefs and values on which I'd based my work had been held up for a viewing, and I did not like what I saw.

I had to ask myself: How genuine was I about changing society for kids? Or was I just in it for a job, given the lack of any perceived alternatives? One thing was obvious. If I was truly on about creating opportunities for the alienated, then I had to do something significantly different.

What I had experienced in that four-day workshop had profound effects, not only for me but also for the other participants. We had started out on the Thursday night with 150 fairly reserved and suspicious strangers. By Saturday afternoon, there was a room full of people with their arms around each other, singing 'Heal the world'.

My question was: How the hell did the organisers do that? I had been working with people for a very long time, and I had never seen anything like this before. I was interested in the technology of how they did what they did. I thought it could be of benefit to my work. I sure as hell had never been able to shift a group of young people like that. Now, I know it was not necessarily long-lasting or sustainable change, and anyone who thought it was the answer to all their human suffering would be disillusioned later, but my question remained, how did they do it? I had experienced change, so I knew it was possible. I had always suspected as much, and now I knew. So, like about one-third of the other participants, I went back to check it out. As a bare minimum most if not all of the participants had realised they had far more choice about determining their own situation. Even if they chose to do nothing about it, they could if they were willing to pay the price.

As for me, I told myself that I was not looking for further personal growth, but simply trying to figure it out. I was still pretty much up that river in Egypt. I was well received by the network of graduates, which was a significant group in both number and calibre, all committed to making the world a better place as well as to working on their own growth and development. This was a whole new world to me. The company that promoted the workshop was called the Wilson Jordan Group, and the two principals were a married couple, Stan and Jane Jordan (née Wilson).

Stan and Jane were dynamic people, completely obsessed with the notion of changing the planet for the better and making a quid in the process. I liked them a lot and they liked me. There was a high-octane energy around the group. They had twenty or thirty people coming in at all hours of the day and night, volunteering to help them grow their business. Everyone was there for their own reasons. As I said, I was there to figure out how they did what they did with a view to learning something that could be useful in my work (still paddling). Others were there because it was the only place on earth where they felt valued or loved for who they were.

I spent about six months around the place, becoming increasingly disillusioned with the welfare system. What was I going to do? Quit? Give up? Maybe I could do something different? Maybe I could sell real estate? Maybe not.

At work, I spent those six months throwing a tantrum. If I was dissatisfied with my work before, now it was unbearable, and so was I. I became increasingly isolated. My complaining was testing the patience of even those closest to me.

'Is this the best we can do?' I kept asking. 'Provide a failing and ever-decreasing welfare system to people? I don't think so.' On and on I went.

One day I was in a pub with one of my new friends, Keith Matson, and he reached across and grabbed a beer coaster on which he wrote 'Passion vs Fear'. He said, 'Paul, until your passion or your desire to do something is greater than your fear, you are not going to do anything. So in the mean time, will you shut up?' He continued, 'If by any chance your passion does exceed your fears, then give me a call. I will do whatever I can to help out. By the way, it's your shout.'

Damn, there I go again into a state of turmoil. Keith was right. I just hadn't seen it like that before. I was indeed scared to do something different, but I didn't know what to do.

Do something was my answer. The worst that could happen would be that I could learn something. Stuff it, I thought, I'll set up my own organisation outside the welfare system. I'll show those bloody youth workers, I'll show the government. I'll prove that it's possible for young people, regardless of their background – that if they have the desire they can turn their lives around and be successful. Yes, that's what I'll do.

So I tentatively announced to a small, select group of people that what I thought I might do er was er maybe soon what I was gunna do was er . . .

My resolve was far from convincing even to me. I ummed and ahed for another couple of months. I created as many distractions as I could in order to avoid doing anything concrete like quitting my job or setting up a company.

I even got married. Sharon and I decided to get married, and after a wonderful ceremony in the Japanese garden at the Royal Melbourne Zoo, we departed for a honeymoon in the Caribbean. I wanted to take Sharon to some of the islands

I had been to five years earlier. I wanted to do this because, although I'd asked her to come along the first time and she had accepted, she got a better offer and went to Greece instead.

So there we were, lying on the beach in Barbados, quietly sipping rum and coke, with the sound of the Atlantic rollers crashing on the sand, calypso music and laughter in the background. The perfect backdrop to paradise. Ah, at last. Peace and quiet. Lying beside my beautiful princess on one of the most idyllic beaches on one of the most beautiful Islands on the planet. I could relax at last and rid myself of the turmoil that had been inside my head and my heart for the past eight months.

Slowly Sharon raised herself up on one elbow, looking magnificent in the new bathing suit she had to have if she was going to the Caribbean. She looked at me lovingly and with her free hand raised her designer sunglasses and said, 'So what are you going to do about it, Paul?'

Ahh, was there absolutely no escape? What could I say?

We discussed at length the implications for us if I were to set up an organisation that would provide real opportunities and training that would enable young people to begin to discover their true worth. The first and most obvious question was the money. 'Simple,' Sharon said. 'You resign from your job, I'll stay on, and my money will support us both until it gets established. If what you create is of significant value, it will attract the support you need.'

Now I could begin to see how it could really happen–and, besides, I was rapidly running out of excuses. It was agreed. When we got back to

Melbourne I would give three months notice and start setting up a company that would best suit our needs.

We arrived in Melbourne on a Sunday and I was back at work the following day. As luck would have it, there was a regional managers' meeting with the Executive Director scheduled for 11.30 a.m. So in I waltzed after six weeks in the Caribbean, feeling pretty relaxed. I couldn't believe what I had walked back into. The bitching and lobbying and squabbling for each other's territory – mainly mine in my absence – with everyone trying to increase their own regions at the expense of other workers, of the organisation and–God forbid to mention it–of the client group.

I can't stay here for three months, I thought. So when it came my turn to say something, I said, 'I quit. I am out of here. Thank you very much, here are the keys, goodbye.' I certainly got their attention–not that I suspect a couple of them gave a toss. They just began the process of carving up my region in earnest.

I went home and told Sharon what had transpired. After a couple of wide-eyed blinks, she said: 'Fair enough. You had better get on with it, then.'

The next day I went in and told Stan Jordan what had happened. He roared laughing and said, 'Well, son, there is a desk, there is the phone. You had better get on with it, then.' And with that I did. Breaking the Cycle was born.

5
Passion vs Fear

So much happened in those first three months. I knew I had to set the bar high and keep to a tight timeframe if I was to realise my dream of creating a model that changed the existing paradigm of working with alienated young people. If I didn't, I'd lose the sense of excitement that was necessary to inspire people to get involved, and any momentum I had gathered would be lost. What we were about to create had to be worth getting out of bed for, both for the potential supporters and for the young people destined to participate in the program.

If it was going to happen, it had to happen now. I boldly declared that in twelve weeks time I would be 'out of here' with twelve young people on a program that would change their lives forever. I needed to inspire people in a way that would put some mass around what was essentially just a good idea and a bucket load of passion At this stage it wasn't a particularly well-developed idea, but my determination to make it happen seemed to make up for that. Besides, there was no turning back now. I couldn't go back to the welfare industry anyway, because no-one would have me.

So, with no more than my borrowed office, borrowed phone and borrowed desk, I set about to create what became the most successful organisation of its kind in Australia. Within two years we were running pre-employment programs in three States and servicing young people and employers from every State and Territory. More importantly, 97 per cent of the young people who entered the program graduated into pre-negotiated jobs, and after six months some 85 per cent were still employed and adding value to their workplaces. Actually, I maintain that the other 15 per cent didn't learn any less. Many of them returned to study, and a couple I know of are now making a great contribution as youth workers.

We achieved all this while working with some of the most alienated young people in the country.

But where could I start? As I said, all I knew was that I was going to create a program that would transform the lives of those game or desperate enough to do it. I thought I would have a look around at what was working and develop my program from there. No rocket science for me.

One of the great advantages of sitting in my borrowed office–which had just enough room for the desk and a three-drawer filing cabinet–was the flow of human traffic that had to pass my door to get to the Wilson Jordan Group. Those who recognised me were curious about what I was up to, so I told them. With those I didn't know, I would invariably strike up a conversation that gave me a chance to enrol them in what was rapidly becoming my vision of the future. With each conversation I would strengthen my resolve, and as each day passed I was able to add a new piece to the quickly developing mosaic that I'd called Breaking the Cycle.

I was passionately convinced that, whatever program we created, it was going to work. At one level, the program content was almost secondary to the context or the environment we were creating – an environment of possibility, one where there were high expectations of everyone involved, and in particular of the young people. I was going to prove the adage, 'you get what you expect'. I suppose one of the reasons for our success was that my commitment and enthusiasm were contagious. All my 'talking it up' meant that the first program was beginning to look more of a reality each day. It also brought in other people's great ideas, encouragement and support, not to mention the much-needed volunteers.

There was so much to do. I didn't have anything. A company structure, a program, money, young people–hell, I didn't even have a business card. Yet, despite all that, I knew it was happening, and the momentum was gathering. Among the great people who volunteered to work with me were Elle Bardas and Lee Deane, who worked tirelessly doing whatever was required to make things happen. Without them, the first program would never have got off the ground. Elle was only 21 years old, but she took no prisoners in her pursuit of her goal. She committed herself to the organisation full-time and became a true source of inspiration as well as a fantastic role model for the other young people, many of whom were older than her. Meanwhile, Lee was helping us to put an office together whenever she could come in. Organisational systems were on my 'yet to be discovered' list, although I did think the concept had merit

Lee was also instrumental in helping to organise the very first fund-raising event for Breaking the Cycle. It was a dinner and auction evening at a pub in North Melbourne owned by José and Sandra D'Olivia, both graduates of 'Money and You'. Lee organised a mailout to the 3500 people on the Wilson Jordan database. It was $40 per head, which in 1992, viewing the world through my welfare mentality, I thought was a big ask. But RSVPs came in thick and fast. Soon it looked as if we would have between 50 and 80 people turn up. From memory we were going to make about $10 per ticket, plus whatever we made on the donated auction items.

One RSVP came in with a cheque for $40 and a message wishing me well but refusing to come to the auction night. Unsociable bugger, I thought. Still, hey, thanks for the forty bucks!

Lee looked at the cheque. It was from a man called Vic Delosa. Holding it up, she called across the room, 'I think you should meet this guy. He's a friend of my brother's, and I reckon you two would get on well.'

'Well, he had his chance to come and he blew it,' I replied flippantly. I was too busy to meet anyone else, particularly if they weren't prepared to come to the auction night.

The night passed. It was a great social event and we looked as if we had raised around $5000, though $3000 of it was still to be collected. The only problem was that I still hadn't paid José and Sandra for the meals. I had assured them I would settle on the night, and by my 'back of the envelope' calculations we had 85 people at $30 each. That made the bill $2550. It wasn't looking good. If we were lucky we might have collected that much on the night, making Vic Delosa's previously banked $40 the gross profit to date.

Sandra looked at me with a soft smile. She said, 'Don't worry, Paul, this is our gift to the kids. We know you will do well with them. Good luck.' My eyes began to fill with tears, and the air in my lungs expanded so much I thought my chest was going to burst. I could not believe the generosity of these two wonderful people. Without being asked, they were donating the equivalent of $2500, not to mention working all night serving 85 guests for the privilege of doing so. My eyes met Sandra's, and I mouthed a 'thank you'. She smiled and gave me a hug that will stay with me forever.

*

At this stage, I had not got down to the finer details of the program. Then one afternoon I was talking to Stan Jordan. Leaning well back in his chair with his hands clasped firmly behind his head, Stan said, 'I reckon you ought to meet Terry Molloy. He's good with kids.' I made a couple of cursory enquiries and learnt that Terry was a facilitator with a youth program called Discovery Australia, which was mainly aimed at younger teenagers who were still at school. I had known a couple of teenagers who had attended Discovery, and I had only heard great things about it. The problem was that it had been set up as a ten-day residential program in the school holidays, and it cost over $1500 to attend. Well worth it, but that kind of thing was hardly going to meet the needs of the young people to whom

I was committed.

I called Terry Molloy anyway. He was in New Zealand at the time, facilitating a Discovery program. We spoke briefly and made arrangements to meet when he returned.

At our first meeting I don't think either of us could believe what we had struck. Terry arrived looking immaculate in a navy-blue jacket with a diamond-studded dollar sign on the lapel, a blue shirt, silk tie and beige dress trousers. I, on the other hand, was in my jeans and an old jumper, looking more like a street kid than a budding program director.

Terry strode confidently into my office, put his briefcase on the floor, shook my hand with a vice-like grip and proceeded to interrogate me.

'So what do you want to achieve in this program?' he began.

'Er, I want to create a program that will change the lives of the participants forever.'

'Yes, I know that, but specifically, what outcomes do you want to achieve?'

'Er, I want to, er, do something that will be long-lasting and will give young people the chance to turn their lives around.'

I could see Terry wasn't impressed. He remained polite, but his face was tightening with each response I gave. It was becoming painfully obvious to both of us that I didn't have a clue about the specifics of the program.

What I did know was the broad framework of what I wanted, and this was largely based on what I had seen work in the past. For example,

I knew wilderness experiences could be of profound value. Outdoor education programs across the world were testament to that. I had witnessed the power of such programs at first hand through the South Port Youth Service, only to see most of the wide-eyed, enthusiastic campers return to the same environment and behaviours immediately on their return. This raised the question, so now what? Wilderness experiences were not enough by themselves. Some argue you can never take that experience away from people, but in my observation it was not enough to produce sustainable change.

I had also personally experienced a process called 'The Game', which was based on a Transactional Analysis framework and facilitated by an extraordinary couple, Ken and Jane Windes. The whole aim of 'The Game' was to invite people to accept that, whatever your own behaviours, whatever you thought of yourself or others thought of you, you were in fact OK – and, more the point, so was everyone else.

From this position of 'OK-ness', you were then invited to look at your own behaviour through the observations and feedback of the other twenty or thirty program participants. It was like having a giant 360-degree mirror held up so you could have a look at your behaviour. Sounds simple enough, and it is, but do you think people generally like what they see? 'The Game' was a powerful process that could lead people into extremely useful personal insights, but where did we go from there?

I was gradually working towards a program that incorporated a range of proven methodologies within our own unique environment and context.

It had to be a model that would attempt to meet the complex and varied needs of young people. It was essential to create a support system, not just for a few short weeks but for as long as it took young people to literally break the cycle of whatever was happening in their lives that was preventing them from realising their potential.

As with most successful models, Breaking the Cycle was organic in nature. While the personnel and program content changed from time to time, the one constant throughout was the environment of the organisation, which in essence was about demonstrating our vision and core values.

Although I felt I'd been grilled by Terry Molloy, or Tezza as he was known, I took an instant liking to him. More importantly, I knew he could make a huge contribution to the life-skills side of the program – and he sure did. Tezza was a chiropractor by profession, and he had studied the latest educational methods from all around the world. I knew I personally could learn a great deal from him; I just didn't know quite how much.

When it came to facilitating programs, I was in a state of being 'unconsciously incompetent', as Tezza would put it: I didn't know what I didn't know. This is often a very dangerous place to be. When you discover what you don't know, then you progress to being 'consciously incompetent'. Well, that's a relief! In fact it *IS* a relief, because now at least you can recognise what you need to learn and why. The aim is to progress to being 'consciously competent' – that is, you are able to complete a skilled task as long as you are thinking about it – through to being 'unconsciously competent', which is doing what you need to do without having to think about it.

Got it!!

Boy, did I have a lot to learn! And learn I did. Tezza took me to meet two of the directors of Discovery Australia, and after hearing what I was going to do, they gave Tezza and Breaking the Cycle permission to use large sections of their tried and tested curriculum for the life-skills component of the program. It was obvious to all of us that, given the target group I was working with, my program was never going to compete with theirs.

We were about six weeks into the process and the program was taking shape. I had approached Graham Scott, an old mate of mine and Troppo's, to lead us in a twelve-day wilderness trek. At the end of it, we would be delivered safely to a team of enthusiastic volunteers under the direction of Tezza and his friend and colleague Rose Witherow, where we would enter stage two of the program, the life-skills residential. But I hadn't recruited any young people yet.

I had also approached an ex-colleague in the Victorian Office of Youth Affairs for a financial contribution, and she had said they'd look into it. So I thought I had better get on with recruiting some young people. After making a few calls to some old youth-worker mates, I went around to see Henry Nissen at the Open Family Foundation.

Henry is a living legend, an icon of youth work in Victoria. Everybody loved him, though he could be infuriating to work with at times. He had been working on the streets of South Melbourne, St Kilda and the city for fifteen years that I knew about. Someone once said affectionately of Henry that 'his heart was so big, it nearly squashed his brain'. Whatever anyone asked of Henry he would always do his utmost to deliver, often at great personal expense. He was without peer when it came to those who were actually trying to do something about the situation of young people in a practical, hands-on way.

Like Henry, the Open Family Foundation was far from orthodox in its approach. Its founder, and Henry's boss, was Father Bob Maguire. Father Bob would provocatively refer to the homeless and alienated as 'the great unwashed, the discards of society', and often suggested that society had given up on these people. I couldn't have agreed more.

When I told Henry and Father Bob of my plans, they offered their support. Father Bob said, 'Well, it is good to see someone having a red-hot go, not like them other parasites' – meaning the youth-work fraternity. Bob was never one to mince words. He added, 'If I back you, don't stuff it up, fer Christ's sake. I'm in enough shit as it is.' And with those encouraging words, Henry and I went out to recruit young people for the first Breaking the Cycle program.

I went out with Henry on the Open Family bus, which did the rounds each evening like a soup van for the homeless. What an experience! It was a long time since I had been on the streets – not since my early days in Carlton. Things hadn't improved any. In fact, life appeared a lot harsher for the growing number of urban refugees. I also noticed that the kids Henry was dealing with now were much younger than the kids I had been seeing some ten years earlier – and almost without exception they were off their faces with one drug or another.

Henry did the introductions. If Henry said I was all right, then that was it. I was all right.

I began asking kids whether they were happy living the lives they were leading. If they said yes, either because of bravado or because they genuinely meant it, then I would say, 'Great! Keep it up, have a nice life.' If on the other hand, as was more often the case, they did not reply or replied in the negative, then I gave them my card and invited them to meet me the next day at my office in Prahran. 'If you're fair dinkum you'll turn up. If not, it's the drugs talking,' I said in what appeared to be a harsh and judgemental tone. 'Either way, it is your life.'

To my amazement a few of them began to turn up, usually in twos and threes. Later I discovered that Henry was out rounding them up and ushering them up the stairs to what must have been the intimidating environment of the corporate office of the Wilson Jordan Group.

Mind you, intimidation cuts both ways. There were some rare sights among Henry's 'great unwashed' – none rarer than a young man who stomped into my office, sat down, put his size 11 laced-to-the-knees bovver boots on my desk and said 'What's all this bullshit about a camp?'

Bloody Henry, I thought. He's been enrolling these guys by telling them I'm taking them on a camping holiday!

I looked at this young man. He had a Mohawk hairstyle with one spike green, the other red, both immaculately glued towards the heavens, making him look six inches taller than he actually was. He was wearing a grungy pair of camouflage pants, and his tattooed arms stuck out of a sleeveless jacket that the op shops would have passed on for rags. I got up, walked slowly around to where he was sitting, gently removed his feet from my desk and eyeballed him.

'It's about respect, you understand?' I said. Then I stuck my hand out and said in a much higher tone, 'G'day. My name is Paul McKessy. Who are you?'

'Grunt.'

I looked at him.

'Grunt, my name is Grunt.'

'Oh, fair enough. So what do you want to know?'

Over the next hour or so, I informed Grunt that this was not strictly speaking going to be a holiday. On the contrary, it could prove to be the toughest thing he had ever done – a three-month program involving twelve days of wilderness trekking, eight days in a residential life-skills program and a follow-up education program.

As with all the other young people who signed on, I told him that the program was about having the opportunity to decide how you wanted your life to be, as opposed to how you thought it had to be. Right from those initial interviews, I was confronting their beliefs about what was possible.

'This is a serious chance for you to get your life on track. Whether you do is up to you,' I continued. 'This first step is making a commitment to having positive changes in your life, making a serious commitment to yourself. If you do that, I will guarantee I will do whatever I can to support you through the process. If you're not prepared to commit to yourself, how can you expect me to? It just won't work. So save us both the trouble and don't do it.' Again I said, 'It's your life – you choose.'

With some, I would throw down the gauntlet and challenge them to do it. With others, it was a matter of helping them to see how things could improve, which seemed to them unlikely given the state of their lives and the evidence they had amassed to the contrary . . . up until now.

The experience of recruiting what turned out to be thirteen young people for the very first Breaking the Cycle program certainly reacquainted me and the team of volunteers with the pointy end of society. Collectively, the participants were all unemployed, and had been for some time. Most had never had a job. More than half were homeless and living on the streets or in squats, half had drug habits of one sort or another, and between them they had racked up more than 200 outstanding charges in the Magistrate's Courts. It was always going to be interesting.

But the program was developing, and young people were beginning to show interest in this crazy idea of making a difference. I had a little bit of money for stamps, tea and coffee. We didn't need much at this stage, as no-one was being paid and we had free rent and phones. The time was getting closer.

As part of enlisting some broader support, I wrote a four-page letter that was a heartfelt appeal to anyone who could be bothered to read it. In it, I asked: 'How would it be if we could change the situation facing so many of our young people, improve the environment and make money doing it?' The letter went on to explain what I was going to do. I wrote: 'I am not about doing welfare better, I am about Breaking the Cycle of welfare dependence.' The letter concluded with an invitation to get involved. The general response was fairly positive, but I didn't expect what happened next.

It was about four weeks before the first program was due to start, and we were all taking 'busy' to a new level. Elle and I were working twelve to fourteen hours a day. Sharon was going to work, then spending four hours with us in the evening.

One morning the phone rang, and I answered. The person on the other end said, 'My name is Vic Delosa and I want to meet with you to discuss the program you are putting together.'

Vic Delosa? The name rang a bell. Oh, yeah, the unsociable bugger who didn't come to the auction night.

'Er, sorry, mate – look, I'm a bit busy right now. Perhaps when I get back from the wilderness?'

'No,' he replied calmly but with great clarity, 'I want to meet with you now.'

'Well, listen, mate, I am serious when I say I am busy. The only time I could meet with you this side of the program is at seven in the morning' – thinking this would be bound to fob off the stranger on the phone.

'Right, then. I'll see you in the morning, 7 a.m.'

I couldn't believe it. I could hardly refuse now, so we arranged to meet at the coffee shop directly under my office.

Sure enough, next morning he turned up at the coffee shop – a stranger in a navy-blue suit with the obligatory red silk tie. After we had exchanged cursory pleasantries and ordered the essential heart-starter, he looked me square in the eye, with purposeful clarity. He reached into his briefcase, produced the four-page letter I had written and proceeded to read it out aloud as if I had never seen it before.

I was sitting there impatiently, my mind running through all the things I had to do in my office upstairs.

Then as he was reading my letter tears began to well up in his eyes. I thought, bloody hell, what have I struck here?

Almost as if he heard my thoughts, he stopped reading and said, 'Listen, mate. I am the managing director of a multinational company. I earn $100,000-plus a year, I have a beautiful wife, three gorgeous sons, two BMWs and a house in Brighton, and I am letting you know that this is not it for me. I want to do what you are doing. I want to be your partner.'

I couldn't believe my ears – partner in what? I didn't have anything to partner in, and the last thing I needed was somebody else to bloody worry about. I said pretty much all that and suggested that he find some way of being involved that would work for him and would be of value to us.

He said, 'I don't think you heard me, mate. I want to be your partner. I want to do what you do.'

I shot back, 'Then you had better do what I did. Quit your job and put $10,000 on the table.' I thought that would cure him.

Without flinching, Vic placed the letter carefully on the top of the pile of papers in his briefcase, rose to his feet and said, 'I'll see you here at 7 a.m. tomorrow.'

'We'll see,' I muttered.

All day the conversation played on my mind. Maybe I should have been more compassionate with the guy. He was obviously as passionate about the plight of young people as anyone I had met, including myself. Lee Deane's words were still echoing in my memory, 'You should meet this guy, I think you two would really get on well.'

Sure enough, he was there at 7 a.m. the next day, two more strong cappuccinos at the ready. Without saying a word, he reached down and produced my letter. Silently he began to read over my words, and once more tears were steaming from his eyes and his lips were quivering uncontrollably.

I thought, bloody hell, here we go again – and once more, as if he had read my thoughts, he took a deep breath and collected himself somewhat. Then, to my amazement, he reached into the inside pocket of his navy-blue suit jacket and produced a chequebook, then wrote a personal cheque to Breaking the Cycle for $10,000.

The first words he uttered were: 'I have spoken to my wife and my employer. I finish work at the end of the month.'

I couldn't believe what I was hearing. It looked as if I had myself a partner whether I liked it or not. I certainly liked it, but I didn't exactly know what he had just become a partner in.

I said, 'Fair enough, then. Welcome to the team. Oh, by the way, thanks for the forty bucks. You missed a good night.'

6
Let the Games Begin

Day One, Program One. Naively, we had set a 9.30 a.m. start. For two full days before – not to mention the previous six months – a team of about a dozen volunteers had been training for this moment.

The room looked fantastic, and everything in it had a purpose. From the very moment you walked in, it was obvious that this was going to be different. From our choice of a pillarless room, so that everyone had an uninterrupted view of the proceedings, to the double flip-chart stand with its colourful sign saying 'Welcome to Breaking the Cycle', it was all there for a reason. Other colourful signs saying things like 'Up until now', 'In the past' and 'Yet' were placed strategically in the young people's line of vision so that whenever they thought they were unable to do something, they'd be reminded that it's what you tell yourself that counts. In the corner was a four-foot blow-up penguin, just content to 'do penguin', a subtle metaphor for accepting yourself for who you are. A large blow-up pterodactyl was suspended from the ceiling, later to be used a metaphor for controlling negative self-talk or internal dialogue.

The young people must have wondered what the hell they had struck – or they would have, if they had been there. At 9.30 a.m. one young person was there. At 10 a.m. there were two and by 10.30 a.m. a grand total of three. I was very tense. What if they didn't turn up? Would everything we had done be wasted? I felt like someone who was trying to throw the best party in town, only to have no-one come. All the what-ifs in the world were raging through my mind. I still don't know exactly what happened, but I suspect Henry Nissen was out there rounding them up, and as he found each person, the room began to fill.

We finally got going around 11.30 a.m. and didn't finish until 9.30 that night. The program was full-on. It had to be. We had decided if we were to retain the interest and commitment of these worldly young explorers, then we had to go at it full tilt – no room for the faint-hearted.

The pace was hectic. Every fifteen or twenty minutes the format would change. This was certainly not going to be confused with going back to school. Just when they'd made themselves comfortable sitting down, we would be up doing a line dance. Then they were lying on the floor considering the qualities they felt made someone a best friend. It was fast, it was slow, it was rowdy, it was intimate. By the time they left the room on that first night, a group of thirteen strangers with street cred and attitude to burn were sitting on the floor with their arms around each other, singing 'That's What Friends are For'.

It was unbelievable, and they loved it. They didn't want to leave. We were still ushering them out at 10.30 p.m. We had succeeded in creating an environment of love and support of a kind that most of them had never experienced before. For the first time, they gave themselves permission to get in touch with who they were and what they truly wanted in life. The bullshit and bravado were left at the door.

I knew it. I knew it. It could be done. If you provided the environment, safety and trust, the invitation and the permission, young people – regardless of their background, their pain, their fears – would show their true colours, their brilliance, their unique qualities, their ambitions. I bloody knew it!

Now it was time to go to work.

Day Two. They all turned up, and from that moment I knew we were to succeed. The only question was how? Day Two was pretty much more of the same. Tezza and the team were brilliant. Not only was everyone engaged actively, but we were all having fun. The first two days were designed to introduce the young people to useful concepts such as how to assume responsibility for their thoughts, feelings, behaviours and actions. We also talked about integrity, and about building trust by only making agreements you are willing to keep, keeping the ones you make, and cleaning up the ones you break.

While some of the teachings were didactic, the lessons were always made interesting by using colours, music and experiences to reinforce the message. We were challenging entrenched beliefs and attitudes, and that was part of what it was about. One of our main targets was the belief, shared by many of these young people as a result of negative school experiences, that they were not capable of learning much, or that they were stupid. In turn they would often rubbish learning or education, saying it was irrelevant. I knew from my own experience how easy it was to adopt that belief, and how limiting it could be. I also knew there was little point just telling people they were capable; they had to experience it for themselves. We were not only interested in teaching new skills, but in teaching them about the process of learning itself.

We broke that process down into five broad 'chunks'. In order to maximise your learning capacity, you need to have the **BELIEF** you can learn; the **WILLINGNESS** to learn; the appropriate **ATTITUDE** required for learning; a willingness to **CO-OPERATE** with others, be they teachers or other learners; and an ability to **BREAK DOWN LARGE OR DIFCULT TASKS.**

To illustrate, we asked the group how long it would take them to learn the relatively complex task of juggling three balls. The responses ranged from a couple of weeks to never. We asked how many would be willing to consider using the five keys to learning to approach the task. That way, we said, you could learn how to juggle three balls in about four hours.

'No way, I don't think so,' was the reply.

With some coaxing, we were able to enrol them into believing that they could learn and being willing to give it a go. And, sure enough, in less than four hours each and every participant had learnt how to juggle, with various degrees of competency.

This process was a powerful metaphor for how human beings all learn differently. Some prefer to observe or to be shown, some need to be told in minute detail, some need to physically do it. No one way of learning is any better or worse that any other; it is just a matter of discovering which suits you best. By co-operating, by giving each other feedback and support, we could all learn something. What a concept!

Simply providing information and expecting people to learn is of very limited value, and yet until very recently that is exactly how the education system was teaching kids. I maintain that for years the problems experienced by so many children in schools have not been their 'learning disabilities' but a systematic 'teaching disability'. If information alone was all you needed, who on earth would smoke a cigarette? It says it right there on the packet, after you have paid your money: this thing is going to kill you!

Once these guys realised they were capable of learning and experienced a brief insight into their preferred learning style, you had to get out of their way. They were excited. A new world of possibility began to unfold. When one of them got stuck and began saying, 'What's the point? I could never do that!' we would retort, 'Up until now' or 'In the past', pointing to one of the colourful posters on the wall.

We told our young explorers: 'If you think you can, you can. If you think you can't, you can't. Either way, you're going to be right.' The future is not just an extension of the past. If you want to have a different outcome or result in life, does it make sense to continue to do what you have been doing up until now? We talked about the keys to success: 1. Know what you want. 2. Take some action – do something. 3. Check your result. 4. Be flexible 5. Persist.

We reminded them of a famous address that Sir Winston Churchill gave to a group of students at an English university. The topic was 'Success'. After someone else had given a ten-minute expansive introduction, Sir Winston walked slowly to the centre of the huge auditorium, placed both hands on the podium, leant forward and said, 'Never, never, never give up.' And with that he returned to his seat.

Our first task was to convince these guys that it was possible for them to assume control and responsibility for their lives. We had to persuade them that with positive support – some would call it unreasonable support, because we would not quit on them or take a backward step when things got hard – they could tackle their demons, make significant decisions about how they truly wanted their lives, and begin the step-by-step journey of heading in a direction of their choice.

I reminded them of a saying of the American author Dr Wayne Dyer: 'You will see it when you believe it.' I said, 'Think about it. How are you ever going to achieve anything if you don't think it possible?' Now, I was the first to admit that up until now, these young people had not amassed a lot of evidence to suggest that positive change was possible. I knew that. But our starting point was to challenge their entrenched belief that it was impossible. From that point, we could then invite them to decide what they wanted in life and have the courage to make a commitment to themselves, to go for it.

The sad truth is that for many of these young people this was the first time anyone had ever asked them to assume responsibility for their lives or convinced them that they were capable of learning how to do it, let alone being successful. Probably they needed to be at a point where they were ready and able to hear it.

The first two days were about learning some new concepts, and the next twelve days were about going bush and checking them out. We said, 'Don't believe us about this stuff, go check it out for yourself.' So they did.

*

We learnt a few lessons before we even got off the bus – in fact, before we even got *ON* it. I had made it abundantly clear that if anyone was not at the designated meeting place by 10.30 a.m. they would be left behind. If they were late, I'd take it that they were resigning from the program.

It was early days, and I wasn't exactly confident that they *COULD* be there by 10.30 a.m., but I knew that I had to increase the gradient of expectation if we were to be fair dinkum. If this program was going to be successful in the long run, those participating in it had to want it and need to be in it more than the program or I needed them to participate. In fact, at this stage it was very much line-ball, but I wasn't going to let them know that. I also made it clear that it was their responsibility to be there on time, not Henry's!

Amazingly, they were all on time – early, in fact. But there was no bus. Bugger. I'd been so busy hammering the participants about responsibility that I'd forgotten to give the bus driver some of the same.

So there we were, stuck in a carpark in Prahran – and what a sight! You'd think you had wandered into the bar scene from **STAR WARS**. Thirteen young people in various degrees of grunge, a couple of GI Joe impersonators ready for their apocalyptic adventure, and half a dozen very nervous volunteers wondering what the hell they had gotten themselves in for.

Then up rolled the bus. The looks on everyone's faces were something to behold. I had omitted to tell them I had borrowed the bus from a mate of mine. It was one of the old square box-type buses that were used by the Spastic Society, complete with a ramp at the back door. Oh, yes, and it was about 40 shades of yellow.

'I'm not getting in that.'

'No way.'

'You've got to be joking!'

'Shame job.'

'No way!'

Gees, it was a funny sight! These hard-arsed street kids, all refusing to get into the ex-'spastic' bus. Obviously a lesson in humility was being offered here.

After much whingeing and groaning, they all traipsed into the bus. I was pretty sure they'd keep a low profile until we cleared the city limits.

By now it was almost noon. We were one-and-a-half hours behind schedule, and ahead of us was a six-hour drive to the Hattah-Kulkyne National Park in the northwest corner of Victoria.

'Let's go,' I urged.

The bus groaned as we rolled out of the carpark. Friends and supporters were cheering and taking the odd photo. I was looking around for Sharon – the only one apparently missing from the crowd.

We were almost out of first gear, some twenty metres away and travelling at eight kilometres an hour, when Sharon came running out of the office, shouting, 'Wait! Wait!' Bloody hell, I thought – will we ever get out of here? But, given that she was my wife and I am not a totally stupid person, I asked the bus driver to pull up.

Sharon was waving an envelope in the air. She said, 'I thought you would like to see this!' and produced a cheque for $10,000 from the Office of Youth Affairs. It was the response to our request some six weeks before, and boy did we need it! I'd been heading out with these guys, committing money we didn't have, assuming that either it would arrive while we were out bush or I would handle it when we got back. I knew that if we hadn't started planning a program until the money arrived, we would still be back at first base. What a relief!

I hugged Sharon, and at last we were off. My spirits were buoyed by the arrival of the cheque and the fact that we had a full crew. Well, that kept me going until lunch. After two or three hours we decided we were a safe enough distance from Melbourne, so we stopped for lunch, which was well overdue given that it was close to 3 p.m.

It was to be a quick stop. Grab a sandwich, have a pee and back into it. No worries, I thought.

Everything seemed to go smoothly. Then, about an hour or more into our second leg, we were cruising along at our maximum 80 kph when we were pulled over by the police, with lights flashing and sirens blaring.

'Shit!' was the collective expletive, followed by some less than complimentary remarks from the back.

I turned to everyone and said, 'Now shut up, we don't know what they want and I don't want anyone making it any worse than it is.' I think they got the point: this was not the time to be pushing any boundaries.

A typical country sergeant-type policeman stepped up onto the first step of the bus and asked, 'Who's in charge of this outfit?'

'I am,' I replied, realising no-one else was about to volunteer.

'How many have you got in your group?'

'Thirteen plus three staff,' I said, wondering if by any chance we were overloaded.

'Are you sure? Do you want to count them?' said Mr Plod.

I counted, then counted again: I could only get fourteen, staff included. When I was counting for the third time, he said, 'The others are in the back of my car and they are not very happy with you'. Bloody hell! We had left two of the girls behind at the lunch stop.

Everyone except me, the police and the two young women concerned thought it was a great joke. We had been travelling for over an hour and no-one had missed them at all. Sometimes it doesn't pay to be quiet.

I explained to the cops who we were and what

we were about. They rolled their eyes and wished me good luck in a manner that suggested I was going to need it.

So on Day One of the wilderness expedition, before we had arrived, I had a personal chance to demonstrate another of our key program concepts: when you make a mistake, it is the opportunity to make a correction and learn from it. From that point on, a headcount was a mandatory ritual before and after every event and session in the bush. In fact, everyone was given a number – staff included – and the person leading the group would call 'circle up'. When we did, they would say 'Count off' and we did – one, two, three . . . If anyone was absent, it was obvious by the silence at their number, not only that someone was missing but also who it was. This ritual became quite an incentive for people to ensure they kept their agreement to be on time for every event or session. I have the dubious honour of being the only Breaking the Cycle staff member ever to lose a participant.

*

Eventually we arrived at our destination and hurriedly set up camp. Our illustrious wilderness leader, Graham Scott, told us what was required for a comfortable night's sleep. As I was about to realise, this was indeed an experiential learning program. If I had been a participant, I would have been asking for a definition of the word 'comfortable' by Day Three.

But the wilderness was a fantastic place to experience life in a concentrated form. It was all well and good for us to espouse the value of co-operation and teamwork in the abstract, but it was far more powerful at the end of a day when we'd done 25 kilometres canoeing. First we debriefed the girls, who innately used the skills of respect, listening and co-operation among themselves. We sat around the campfire with a hot cuppa and talked about how they'd managed to enjoy a relaxed paddle, set up their tent, cook dinner in daylight, and still have half an hour or so to chill out before our evening meeting.

We then turned to the boys, who were still blaming each other because they had paddled an extra ten kilometres on the same river, having taken the bank-to-bank route. They were yelling at each other, the fly on their tent was still not up, and dinner was a mess because they'd taken twenty minutes to decide who was prepared to do what. When we asked these guys to debrief, everyone could see which was the more useful approach. I thanked the guys for giving such a graphic demonstration of what happens when you spend most of the day not listening to each other, blaming each other for what isn't working, justifying the miserable result and wanting to quit. It was very considerate of them to contribute to the team's collective learning. Sarcasm aside, it was true.

Up until now, I haven't mentioned my tent buddy and good mate Keith Matson, the bloke in the pub who had challenged me to put up or shut up with the 'Passion vs Fear' beer coaster. After deciding to put up, I went back to him and reminded him of his offer to help me. He was true to his word, and as for helping – did he what!

Keith had a background in accounting and

corporate law, and had been studying to facilitate personal growth workshops for some time. When I approached him, he said, 'I'd love to help, Paul, but I have got an $800 power bill, and if I don't pay it, they will disconnect my power.'

'Fair enough,' I said. 'Come with me and I'll pay it.' That was probably the best 800 bucks I have ever spent. Apart from a few months here and there, Keith was to be involved with Breaking the Cycle one way or another for the next six years.

As tent buddies, we were like Oscar and Felix in *THE ODD COUPLE*. Keith would meticulously fold every article of clothing and neatly place them on top of each other in one corner of the tent. Meanwhile, I would open the tent flap and throw my stuff inside. Then later I'd be asking him if he had seen my jumper or whatever it was.

Now, the thing about being the messy one is you tend not to notice the neat one's weird behaviour until it is pointed out. Usually this doesn't happen until the neat person has been pushed well and truly past their tolerance level – as in this case.

I hadn't noticed it, but Keith had been moving my stuff over to my side of the tent, usually folding something of mine in the process. About Day Four, Keith politely asked if I would mind not throwing my dirty clothes all over his sleeping bag and his side of the tent.

'Sure, mate,' I said, but I didn't think or do much more about it until about Day Eight, when we had a more focused discussion about the pros and cons of cohabiting in confined and unhygienic quarters. I had no idea that living with me could present so many opportunities to learn tolerance, flexibility and forgiveness.

Keith was a fantastic ally and friend throughout. He was also built like the bus. He had never experienced young people like these before, which was a great strength, because his thinking was not contaminated by previous negative experiences. We spent many an hour discussing strategies, trying to work out how to support one or another of the participants to break through the challenge or demon they were confronting.

The bush itself was fairly boring. Flat desert and miles and miles of dead trees. Having said that, if it had been any more difficult, it might have been too much at this stage of our program's development. All of the young people were seriously challenged, not only by the environment, but also by the dynamics of being in this group. It wasn't just Keith who had to put up with a difficult tent buddy.

Almost every given situation was unfamiliar – making a cup of tea, walking twenty kilometres with loaded packs, canoeing, navigating and of course acquainting oneself with Doug the shovel, a roll of toilet paper and a box of matches. We had deliberately placed people in a situation where they had to rely on others, trust others, co-operate, attempt to understand and communicate. These were the real challenges. The bush merely accelerated the process, because we were removed from the comforts of home and the distractions of life. Some were missing loved ones, others were detoxifying from raging amphetamine addictions. This was no theme park, and we all knew that out there we were playing for keeps.

Thankfully, it was almost as if the participants

all took turns in breaking through their personal challenges. For most, it was a cathartic experience, and I don't know how we would have coped if they all been doing it at once.

I remember one event when my big mate Grunt decided he had 'had enough of all this bullshit', which in reality meant he was doing it hard, and was at a point where he had to break through or give up. I knew and he knew that if he gave up now, he would be going back to a very unsafe existence on the streets with an attitude of 'Fuck the world'. I kept encouraging him, pushing him, letting him know he was capable of working through this stuff and reminding him that he knew what would happen if he didn't.

Meanwhile, Keith was continually confronting Grunt's unacceptable behaviour. It was like watching two rams on the same mound. Finally, Grunt lost it. He took off on a rampage.

Fortunately, all the trees in the desert were dead already. He picked up logs and smashed them, put his size 11 jackboots through huge rotting trunks, yelling and grunting from the pit of his stomach.

Keith and I looked at each other. 'Better the trees than us,' Keith quipped.

This explosive act of destruction lasted for about twenty minutes, until Grunt could grunt no more. He had been storing that rage for most of his twenty years.

Respectfully, I approached him and asked, 'How do you feel?'

'All right. Bloody good, actually – yeah, bloody good.'

It was a significant choice point in Grunt's life. He had chosen to get on with it instead of getting out of it. Afterwards we spoke for hours about his life, his family, his pain. He had left home at fourteen, unable to relate to his father, despite his obvious love for the man. We recognised that his dad was more than likely doing his best, given what he knew of how to bring up strong-willed, independent boys. Indeed, the only thing Grunt could do much about was how he behaved or related to his dad. He couldn't necessarily change his dad, but he could change how that affected him. That was how he felt, and I agreed – life isn't fair, but it's what you do about the injustice that counts.

One of the questions we would ask the young people was, 'Who is driving your bus?' In Grunt's case, he hadn't seen his family for five or six years, yet the relationship with his father was still driving him every day, in virtually every relationship he had. It was time to do something about it. So began that young man's journey to break the cycle of relationships that were less than what he wanted and deserved. (As a postscript, Grunt reverted to calling himself by his given first name and returned to the Northern Territory about two years later to work with his father in his bricklaying business. For years, his mother regularly sent a small donation to Breaking the Cycle with a heartfelt letter thanking us and keeping us in distant touch with her beautiful son's progress.)

*

We had now been in the bush for nine days. It

felt like nine months. I had never experienced such a marathon emotional roller-coaster, and we had three days to go before beginning the next phase of the gruelling event – Tezza's residential life-skills program. I was seriously wondering if I had bitten off more that we could collectively chew. I had heard the adage about how to eat an elephant – one bite at a time – but this was the McKessy Method of eating an elephant: bite off more than you can chew, then chew like buggery. I was already exhausted, not by the physical demands so much as the emotional and personal challenges.

The wilderness trek was created as a metaphor for life. So, as with life, it was a journey, always moving forward. For the last two days, we had to leave the national park and make our way by mountain bikes back to Swan Hill, our destination for the next part of the program, a hot shower and a bed with a mattress. Given the group's general fitness level, this was no mean feat.

On the first day's ride out of the national park, we confronted a 20-knot headwind and driving rain that was coming horizontally into the riders' faces. Keith and I had taken the bus on ahead to locate a camping spot for the night. Besides, us old blokes needed a break! When the rain began, Keith and I looked at each other. This will pass soon, we thought. We were right except for the 'soon' bit. It bucketed down. It was the sort of weather you wouldn't put a brown dog out in.

Now, among our volunteers was an amazing bloke called Ross Dakin, who had volunteered to help out where he could with the logistical support. Before the program started I didn't know Ross well, so it was a pleasant surprise to discover his practical 'bush skills' and no-nonsense approach. As it turned out, we would have been in real trouble without him.

Ross was a country boy, brought up literally back of Bourke in outback New South Wales. After a couple of days of observing his style, Keith and I nicknamed him 'Digger', a name that has stuck to this day. Everywhere we went, Digger would don his Akubra, meander up to a complete stranger and say 'G'day' in a tone that would do Mick Dundee proud. It was like he was a local. Farmers would open gates for us to camp on their properties near running water. Farmers' wives would appear with fresh scones and cream for all. Whenever we approached anyone or came on a farmhouse, Keith and I would stay in the front seat and watch with amazement while Digger won the confidence of the usually conservative person he was talking with. It was a great effort, especially given the appearance of the yellow spastic bus.

It was Digger who helped us locate a town hall where the bike-riders could shelter from the rain. The hall was about the size of a small classroom, reflecting the population of the town. Though he'd never been in the town before, Digger found where the key was hidden.

I asked him, 'How did you know where the key was?'

He shrugged. 'They're always hidden there.'

We needed to bring in the crew, dry them off and have a well-deserved lunch. Keith and I went back and let them know we had lunch organised and dry clothes laid out for them.

Within an hour or so, everyone dragged themselves in, mostly dropping their bikes in a pile – I thought we were going to be literally breaking the cycles here – and collapsing on the floor exhausted. It was a tender moment.

After everyone had eaten lunch and had a chance to thaw out, I called the group together. Outside, the rain was still bucketing down with strong headwinds. I told them how incredibly proud I was of each and every one of them, of their achievement, commitment, courage and persistence. In a speech worthy of the great Ron Barassi, I told them they had nothing more to prove out here – they had done it. I continued, 'What we have decided to do is to ferry everyone the remaining 25 kilometres to the campsite, where Digger has already got a fire going.'

There was a stunned silence, then someone said, 'Bullshit yer will.'

'No way,' said someone else. 'We haven't come this far to pack it in now.'

I couldn't believe what I was hearing. In solidarity each young person berated me for wanting to quit – to give up.

'You're always telling us quitters never win, Paul. We've got too much at stake to quit now.'

'This isn't about a program, this is about my life,' said one young woman who had spent the past several years battling drug addiction and prostitution.

I was in awe. In that moment, the program and all those involved with it, including me, rose to a whole new level. I could not have stopped them now even if I had wanted to. In virtual silence they all packed up their gear, put on their japaras and helmets and rode off into the rain.

This event brought home to me how much we underestimate the capabilities of young people. I was on the learning team once more!

When the weary cyclists arrived, Digger Dakin had a roaring fire and plenty of sweet, hot tea on tap for them. He had also managed to set up everyone's tents in the most sheltered position available.

That evening we had a huge celebration. It was probably the first time most of the participants could recall being proud of themselves and what they had achieved. I remember thinking if we all went home now, these young people would have got their money's worth. Not that they had any money, of course.

I said to them, 'No-one needs to tell you that you are capable of great things ever again. You know that now. You have had that experience. In fact, when things get tough in your life, as they will – possibly tomorrow – think back to today. Think clearly about what it was you drew on today to achieve this result. Access that and you can do anything.'

We received a warm reception when we arrived at our destination in Swan Hill. Someone had contacted the media, and I appeared on the local TV news looking like I had been dragged through a hedge backwards. Luckily for the viewers, we don't have smell-a-vision.

The response was amazing. People in the street had seen the news, and as we rode through Swan Hill they would applaud and call out words of encouragement. The staff had baked a cake with 'Congratulations – You did it' on the top. The mood was good. Hot showers, good food – cooked by someone else. Ahhh . . . luxury.

*

The next morning at 6.30 a.m. it was up and at 'em, rise and shine. We were back into it. Life skills with Tezza and the team. There are those beaming faces of the support team again, I thought, and now I know why they beam. They are so genuinely enthusiastic about what they are doing – and the contribution they are making to the lives of other people. They can't help themselves. Before long, under the masterful facilitation of Terry Molloy, we were all one big happy family.

Tezza got the young people talking about what had happened during the wilderness trek. He managed to get them to open up about all the great moments, positive and negative alike, and he skilfully drew out the lessons of these experiences, not only for the ones involved but for all of us, staff and volunteers alike. It was great.

The life-skills week was to be a continuation of the first couple of days in Melbourne. While we had been out trekking in the bush, a team of volunteers had converted a disused factory showroom into an almost exact replica of our course room, right down to the positioning of the flip-chart stand, the chairs, the music table – even the bloody penguin was in the same spot. It was as if some one had picked up our course room and transferred in through space to Swan Hill. This helped to splice together all the lessons we'd learnt to date as we progressed in our journey of discovery.

The participants and staff took turns to share the innermost feelings and fears they had experienced out bush. A real intimacy and trust had been developed, and I felt privileged to be part of this extraordinary group of people. We laughed, we cried, we joked, we hugged. Above all, we had created an environment where we felt safe enough to reveal our true selves without the need to lie. And, when all was said and done, we were all pretty much the same, all doing our best to have our needs and wants met. Needs and wants like wanting to be loved and accepted for who we are, to be understood, to be valued and respected. To have enough money in the bank to pay the rent and go to the movies if we want to, to have a job where we are appreciated and where we can make a contribution to the success of the company and in turn ourselves. I don't think anyone was asking a lot. I would find the same thing time and time again over the next eight years with more than 1200 young people.

At the same time, the program was deliberately designed to provoke and challenge beliefs, attitudes and behaviours that were not of use to the person concerned or the group. Spirits were high, and some of the young people's behaviour began to push the envelope of acceptability. On about the third day, after three or four requests for co-operation had had no effect on this restive minority, Tezza walked to the front of the room. As he walked past me, he said, 'Trust me.'

He sat down out the front, and the rowdy

behaviour continued. Then he got everyone's attention in an instant. He said, 'I've been talking with Paul, and we've decided to shut down the program. It is obvious to us that you don't want to be here, and to be honest we have all got better things we could be doing with our lives.'

I nearly died. What the hell are you doing, I thought, almost loud enough for someone to hear. Knowing that I'm not much of a poker player, Tezza looked at me as if to say 'Don't say anything.' He continued, 'This is an adult program designed for young adults who want to get on with their lives. What I see is a bunch of kids behaving like children who don't look as if they want to be here. I think it's a real shame that you have this fantastic opportunity and, rather than go for it, you're behaving like schoolkids on a Year 8 camp. I feel really disappointed about that, and I know Paul is sad that this is it, after all he and Sharon have been through to set this program up, it's come to this.'

You could hear a pin drop in the next street.

'So this is it, guys. I'll tell you what I'm going to do. I'll give you ten minutes to decide if you want the program to continue. If you do, and you can convince Paul it is worth going on, then we will see. If not, we'll pack up and be out of here in an hour.'

With that, Tezza got up and gestured to all the staff to follow him outside – including a flabbergasted Paul McKessy, who could see the fruits of his labour and vision of the future about to hit the fan.

It was a sombre moment. No-one spoke a word.

When we were out of earshot, Tezza said, 'That ought to get them going.'

'Them . . . Them . . . get *THEM* going! What the . . . hell have you done!' I yelled.

'Don't worry about it. Trust me. They need to be here more than you need to have them here, remember.' Obviously in my mind it was still line-ball.

We couldn't hear the content of the screaming match that was going on inside the course room, but it was obvious that the women had decided to step up and take control of the situation.

We were all duly summoned back and lined up in a row at the front of the room. All of the young people were sitting on the floor in front of us – in silence. Then one by one each young person stood up, apologised for how he or she had been behaving and said that they wanted to continue with the program. Some were in tears. As they saw it, their lives were at stake, and they thought they had blown it. Each apologised to me and personally thanked me for putting it on the line for them the way I had. I was in tears as well, like most of the staff, and felt overwhelmed by humility. Another powerful demonstration of the capacity of youth.

After everyone had had their say, Tezza said, 'OK, so it looks like we are back on track. OK with you, Paul? Let's have a ten-minute break and get back into it.' At that the music co-ordinator hit the button, and an appropriate song to change the mood was pumping once more.

Tezza grinned at me. I looked at him and said, 'You bastard! Tell me next time you are going to do anything like that!'

*

Late one afternoon, not long before the life-skills program was due to finish, one of the staff came and told me they had seen a pizza delivery going into the boys' cabin. We were having a break and were due to go back into the course room after dinner for our evening session, which generally finished around 9.30 or 10 p.m.

As part of the contract on which we'd based the program, all the staff members, volunteers and participants had agreed that for the duration of the residential program they would not make or receive phone calls except in an emergency. When people are in the middle of such a demanding and often emotional process, it can cause big problems if they ring home in tears or rage about how they are and what is going on. The person on the other end is completely out of context and can be unnecessarily worried for days, while the person who makes the call is usually fine a few moments later.

The agreement was also designed to prevent distractions. We didn't want participants being tormented and wondering whether to leave or not after hearing of some drama that was going on at home – usually a drama, I might add, that they could do little or nothing about. Anyhow, the agreement was that everyone who signed up was not to use the phone.

When I was told about the pizza delivery, I was really annoyed. After all, I was paying to feed these guys, and I saw it as another push of the boundaries.

As I walked toward the cabin, I could hear shuffle, shuffle, rumble, rumble. I respectfully knocked on the door. It opened, and I was almost knocked over by the aroma of what could only be a large Hawaiian and garlic bread.

I would like to share with you how calmly and rationally I confronted the issue, but I didn't. I spat the dummy. I could justify it by saying I was tired, which I was, but that's no excuse. My dummy was firmly in the dirt.

'What is it with you blokes?' I shrieked. 'When are you gonna get it? I'm paying to feed you, and you're eating pizza.'

I threw my tantrum and left, feeling really lousy about the way I had just mishandled the situation. I thought about it for a while, and I decided this was as good an opportunity as any to demonstrate some of what we had been teaching.

So, just before dinner, I went back to the cabin and said, 'Guys, I'd like to apologise for how I just behaved. I'm sorry. I made a mistake. I could have handled it much better. In fact, I'd like to make sure that I'm not emotionally charged when I handle a situation like that again. So is there anything I can do to make it right with you guys?'

'Nah, don't worry about it, Paul. We shouldn't have done what we did – we're sorry too.'

'No, it isn't OK, fellas. I'll tell you what I will do to make it up to you two in particular' – this to Grunt and another bloke called Damien, the two main culprits – 'I will personally serve you dinner.'

'No, it's OK, it really is.'

'No, I insist.'

So, come dinnertime, the two culprits sat down, and I brought out three bowls of hearty vegetable soup for entree, two or three serves of chops, mash and vegies (with plates piled dangerously high) and a couple of bowls full of custard and apple pie for dessert. I didn't want my boys to go hungry, now did I? We all, including them, thought it was a great laugh.

Then the next session began in earnest. Tezza made sure it was a particularly energetic activity – we didn't wasn't anyone dozing off. Just before 9.30 p.m., Tezza had everyone sitting on the floor and was in the midst of making some announcements about the next day's schedule when in burst the same two pizza delivery men, yelling, 'Pizza for Grunt and Damien! Pizza for Grunt and Damien! Is there a Grunt and Damien in the room?'

To their credit, the two boys rose to the big occasion and downed another two large Hawaiian pizzas. Everyone else shared in the treat, and the two pizza-lovers were last seen heading outside to relieve their overstretched stomachs. Touché.

7
So What Now?

By the time we returned to Melbourne, everyone in the organisation had grown substantially. My belief was that people have the potential for change, as long as you provide them with the appropriate challenge, skills, support and opportunity. Until now, these young people had not amassed much evidence to suggest that their lives could be anything but wasted. I wanted to change that. My essential philosophy was that the future is not a natural extension of the past. However hard it may seem, we are moment by moment making choices that are heading us in a certain direction. But I realised that these young people were not conscious of a lot of their choices. It's not as if they were actively saying 'I want to be unemployed or homeless or addicted to drugs'; life is far more complex than that. The reality, however, was that if they were going to turn their lives around, the impetus had to come from them. The American civil rights activist Jesse Jackson once said to the people of Harlem, 'You may not be responsible for being down but you are responsible for getting up.' This became part of the creed of Breaking the Cycle.

But for me the next few weeks in Melbourne were really tough. I was asking myself, what had we achieved? Most of the Program One graduates had gained employment with a supporter of Breaking the Cycle, but a couple had slipped back into the lifestyle the had previously enjoyed. We had provided the opportunity for thirteen young people to turn their lives around and, yes, the majority had taken up the offer. But at what cost? I and my handful of helpers had committed more than eight months of our lives, heart and soul, and here we were again, with no young people, no jobs and no money. There had to be a better way.

We floundered for a couple of weeks. The first program had taken so much effort and energy that I wasn't sure we could crank it up to do it all again. But crank it up we did. Once more, with more passion than cash, it was a case of 'If in doubt, do something.'

News of our first program's success spread like wildfire, which probably says more about the infrequency of success stories than our marketing abilities. An amazing amount of goodwill and support began to pour in. We had Country Women's Association groups knitting woollen beanies for young people, teams of volunteers conducting 'Fun Runs' to raise money, and other fund-raising events being organised by graduates of the Money and You program. It was very heartening.

Better get on with it, then. We recruited in much the same way as we had for the first program, with two important additions. The first was the assistance of the graduates of Program One, who were seen and heard dragging their friends in the front door, saying, 'Now get your shit together and get yourself on this program.' The other was a woman called Lisa Tehan, who was employed in Frankston to assist long-term unemployed people into employment. Frankston was an area of high youth unemployment, and it had a reputation for being a particularly rough area, despite its magnificent bayside location. Lisa's commitment to her client group was extraordinary, and her efforts were largely responsible for getting almost half of the group to the starting line.

Program Two was tough. The young people who had enrolled had some significant challenges and had yet to emerge and show their true selves. There were young people who had experienced physical, emotional and sexual abuse, and others who had very little sense of their worth. One such young woman was Belinda. Despite being brought up in a loving family and having the privilege of attending private school, Belinda was in deep personal trouble. She had spent the last couple of years in an attempt to find herself and to just be happy. Unfortunately, her journey had taken her into some dark places, and she found herself caught up in a lifestyle that was dominated by drugs. She had effectively checked-out of life. Like the others, Belinda needed to be on this program to kick-start her life again and head it in a direction she wanted, away from the drugs and apathy that had consumed her.

I had decided Swan Hill was too far away, and I had seriously evaluated the length of the wilderness trek, I can assure you. Through a couple of contacts from my earlier days I decided to hold the program in East Gippsland. I subcontracted a wilderness company to deliver us via the bush to our residential destination, Ontos Health Retreat, a magnificent 600-acre organic farm that doubled as a yoga and relaxation center. My brief to the wilderness company was that the trek had to be challenging, and we had to get there under our own steam. But I certainly wasn't expecting what happened next.

After a six-hour bus trip from Melbourne, we settled into our first campsite, which was on the banks of the Snowy River in East Gippsland's high country. The next morning we were ferried upriver to a location near McKillops Bridge. If the planet had a roof, it felt like we were standing on top of it. The beauty of the place was already having a profound effect on some of our more hardened city dwellers.

The group was given enough provisions for the day's hike down the mountain, following the Snowy River back to our campsite. In the briefing we were told we should get back to camp between 2 and 3p.m. Wrong. In fact, it was 30 hours before most of us saw our beds. Our group was no doubt slower than a group of experienced hikers, but we weren't 24 hours slower. Our intrepid wilderness instructors had miscalculated the amount of time the hike was to take.

The first few hours were quite enjoyable. The sun was shining. We had our lunch on a beautiful grassy knoll beside the Snowy, and we were all in awe of the magnificence of the environment.

After lunch it was decided that I should remain at the rear of the group to pick up and encourage the stragglers. About the middle of the afternoon, the serious whining and moaning began. There was one young woman I will call Mel, who in the past month had detoxed from heroin and amphetamines. Mel was not in good shape, but she knew she had to detox to do the program and she knew she had to do the program if she wanted to salvage her life. Belinda had also remained at the back of the pack in order to support Mel. Although they were like chalk and cheese, Belinda obviously felt some affinity for her team mate. I had heard of seminars that help you to get in touch with your inner child. Well, Mel's inner child was out and having a massive tantrum.

As sunset approached, I started to get worried. The only comforting thought was that the campsite was on this river, so we weren't lost; we just weren't there yet. In what seemed like about 30 seconds, dark descended and you could not see much more than the end of your arm in front of you. We were not happy campers.

Over the past three hours, Mel had reached new heights in complaining, sitting down every five minutes refusing to go on. Then, all of a sudden, she realised the seriousness of the situation. 'I fucked up didn't I?' she said.

'I think you did' I replied. 'Still, just another challenge', I said in a tone that failed to even convince myself.

So there we were, two young women and me, stuck out on a ledge above a ravine. No food, no matches, no shelter, pitch black and not dressed for an overnight in the Snowy River high country. It was the longest night I can ever remember. Fortunately, Mel was feeling remorseful enough to stop complaining, which was just as well; I reckoned Belinda would have punched her lights out. We were hungry, more than a little scared, freezing cold and extremely uncomfortable, but our spirits were good.

After a couple of hours it was obvious our rugged wilderness instructors were not going to arrive with a St Bernard and a flask of brandy, so we huddled together and did our best to stay warm. Sitting out there on that ledge, I had a lot of time to think. I was concerned for the others, not knowing if we were the only ones who hadn't made it back. I was concerned about what this might mean for Breaking the Cycle; this was not the sort of publicity it needed at such a delicate stage of its existence. That thought consumed me for hours.

Then another thought occurred to me. What was happening here was a metaphor for what I had been telling our young people. I had been saying, 'There will be many events that occur in your life that you will have little or no ability to control. What you *CAN* control is your response to the event.' I had told them that it was important to respond in a way that would see them learn, grow and be stronger, not to react negatively, blaming everyone else, becoming a victim of the events and those causing them. Reacting can drain your energy, which is why people give up on themselves and go into quit mode for the rest of their lives.

So here I was in the midst of an event that I could do little about. When I remembered my own words, I began to laugh and laugh. I think the two girls were quite worried about me, which was fair enough.

Eventually the sun came up. We were too cold, uncomfortable and hungry to appreciate its magnificence, but it did mean we could get on our way for what we thought would be a short stroll into camp for a hot cuppa and a hearty breakfast.

Wrong again. We walked at a reasonable pace – no whining, just one step after the other – for five hours. I was definitely not a happy camper.

Everyone, including the dynamic duo leading this circus, had been caught out overnight. The pacesetters made it to within three hours of the campsite. We were lucky that no-one had been hurt. Out of earshot of the group, I had a frank and direct debrief with George of the Jungle and his chimp leading the trek.

As a postscript, Belinda went on confronting her dragons. When we set up our own wilderness division, she became one of our best wilderness instructors. I was talking to her recently, and she said the events of that trip had been one of the most significant turning points for her. As for Mel, she was able to remain free of drugs and get out of the sex industry. The last I heard of her she was doing an outstanding job being mum to two young children.

Another memorable incident took place on this program. In the middle of the East Gippsland wilderness in the wee small hours of the night, one young man changed his life for ever, and in doing so played a significant role in the lives of many others.

Phil was referred to Breaking the Cycle by Lisa Tehan. When I first met him, he had made numerous attempts to take his own life, and he had just been released from a private hospital, where he had been medically treated for severe depression. I was torn between compassion for the way his life was, for the obvious pain and torment he felt, and concern that he might not be able to go through the program without further harming himself.

In all my years of working with young people, I had never come across anyone with such an overwhelming sense of sadness and despair. It was as if Phil's spirit had vacated his body. Although he was 6 feet 4 inches tall, he appeared very small, almost invisible. When he spoke, which wasn't very often, he had a deep yet thin voice. I was far from convinced that Breaking the Cycle would be right for him, yet I also had a strong sense without a significant intervention of some sort this young man was likely to kill himself.

Phil knew this better than I did, so despite my fear I decided to allow him to participate, after getting written consent from his doctor and psychiatrist. This was a challenging situation for me. I was torn between Phil's obvious need and my concern for his safety. I was also acutely aware that Breaking the Cycle could ill afford the flak we would cop if he were to harm himself while he was participating. (I had copped criticism from some quarters of the youth work industry before we had even conducted our first program.)

Then it dawned on me that I'd been more concerned about the reputation of Breaking the Cycle and the ramifications for me than for this young man. Once I had this realisation, I knew I had to give Phil the opportunity to salvage his life – but I was still concerned for him.

Fitting in with the other young people was a real challenge for Phil. The rowdy and boisterous behaviour, the aggression and verbal jousts were hard for him to be around. For the first few days of the wilderness trek, he did not say a word. The arguments and conflict among some of the group were unbelievable at times, particularly when things got tough.

About the fourth night, after three days of canoeing, the whingeing and moaning were reaching a peak. It was only about 7.30 p.m. but, being the middle of winter, it felt like about midnight. It was then that Phil exploded. He couldn't contain his rage any longer. He left the campsite holding his head, screaming for everyone to shut up. He could no longer stand the petty bickering and complaints. It reminded him too much of home.

I followed Phil at a respectful distance, letting him know I was there but giving him the space he needed to express his pain. After some time, he stopped screaming and began to cry. He curled up in a ball and cried and cried and cried until he was almost dry retching.

By this time I was by his side holding him and assuring him it was OK to get this stuff out and telling him he was safe.

Phil spoke for a couple of hours. He talked about his schizophrenic mother, who for most of his life was too sick to care for him, and his dad, who coped by going to the pub every night, and how for as long as he could remember he had felt like a complete alien on the planet. He was misunderstood and unable to understand others.

He had spent most of his childhood in a very dark place, feeling alone and scared. He felt constantly put down and in his words 'felt like nothing but shit'. The constant yelling and screaming in his family only drove him deeper into himself and into depression. This outburst was the first time he had spoken up. At one level he had to admit it felt pretty good, yet he had scared himself because he believed he was capable of hurting the others in the group in order to shut them up.

I put it to Phil that right now he was at a significant point of choice in his life.

Raising his head, Phil looked me straight in the eyes for the first time since I had known him. I suspect he thought I was the one who was mad.

I said, 'It is up to you, mate. You can continue to speak up and begin to have a say in how you want your life to be, or you can disappear back inside, having your silent temper tantrum, wishing it were different. Phil, it's up to you. It's your life.'

We continued talking for some time. I suggested this could be one of the best opportunities he was going to get to turn his life around – in fact, given the way his life was, it might be the only chance. 'Choice point. It's up to you. Make a promise to yourself you won't quit or give up on yourself, because, mate, that's probably what it is going to take.'

I also pointed out that he wasn't Robinson Crusoe; this is pretty much how life is for all of us, and we all have to deal with various kinds of challenges or pain from our past. I assured him if he made a commitment to move forward in life, then he could rely on my support for as long as it took.

We spent some time in silence, then I suggested we go back to the camp and Phil take the first step by sharing with the group some of what he told me. I assured him that when he spoke, what he said was worth listening to, but the others wouldn't know that because he hadn't said anything yet.

He was very anxious about speaking. I asked him what he considered more frightening, speaking up or disappearing back inside for ever. Phil knew of the significance of his next decision.

We went back to the campsite, where things were now relatively subdued. I informed everyone that Phil had something to say and that, in keeping with our agreement to be respectful, we should all listen without interruption. What transpired over the next couple of hours was truly inspirational. Phil spoke of his life, and of why he was the way he was. He spoke calmly and with purpose. There was not a person in the group who could not feel the pain and in some way relate it to their own. Those who had been whingeing the most realised they did not have much to complain about.

That night in the middle of the bush, Phil changed his life because he had to. Sure he was going to experience more pain and challenges, but that night he had made a decision to live, and to learn how to enjoy his life. Phil wanted to feel love, respect, happiness, to be content, to feel connected with other people. More than anything else, he wanted to get to know who he really was, instead of always hiding from the pain, suffering and loneliness he had confused with himself.

Over the remaining days of the program, Phil was on a roll. His self-esteem and his standing in the group soared. Whenever he spoke we listened, and what he had to say was generally of value. After the program finished, he decided he wasn't ready for a job yet; instead, he wanted to go travelling around Australia on a journey of discovery. All of us chipped in and bought him a backpack and a farewell cake.

Over the next two years I received the most amazing letters from Phil. Some of them were twenty or more pages in length. His insights into life and his experiences travelling through the Kimberley were extraordinary. There is no doubt in my mind my life is richer for meeting Phil and the hundreds of other unique and wonderful young people like him who, when presented with the opportunity to assume responsibility for their lives, do so with a passion.

8
Spotlight on Youth

Despite the personal gains everyone made during our programs, it was always a challenge to find employers willing to take these young people on. The vast majority had never had a job, and even those who had managed to find jobs hadn't been able to hold them for any time.

We were keen to build our own business, partly to create an independent source of revenue, but also to provide employment for some of our graduates. With the assistance of a few business supporters, Rod Winning, Hank Rosens and Rob Deane, we started Cycle Press, a small printing company, and Cycle Building Services, a building site clean-up crew. Both companies were started without any capital, and with employees who had little or no work experience. They struggled from day one, but they did serve a valuable purpose. They employed about half a dozen of our more challenged graduates, and they helped form the 'can-do' attitude that saw Breaking the Cycle become one of the most successful programs of its type in Australia.

But for us to achieve our aims, we needed another strategy to get employment for our graduates. One day Sharon said quietly, 'Why don't you get the jobs first? That way there won't be such pressure to find them at the end of the program, and no-one will be disappointed.'

What a simple yet profound idea! That one thought shifted the whole way we worked with young people. In hindsight it seems obvious, but it had never been done before.

The concept was simple. I would talk to employers and find out specifically what they were looking for in an employee. Then, when I had convinced enough employers we could supply them with young people with the qualities they wanted, we would recruit the young people into the pre-negotiated positions. Young people who graduated from the program would be deemed to be ready for work, and would commence work directly after the program. The system also acted as a carrot for participants, particularly for those sick of doing pre-employment programs that built their self-esteem, only to remain unemployed upon completion.

A lot of pre-employment programs had a counterproductive effect. Young people would tell me time and time again that they felt totally useless because they still could not get a job after doing program after program. Many of them deduced there must be something seriously wrong with them if they were still being rejected.

As providence would have it, the first employer I went to see was Morry Fraid, the managing director and co-owner of Spotlight stores. Spotlight is an amazing company and a great success story. I had met Morry on a couple of occasions before. We were introduced by a good friend, Peter Dixon, a former general manager of Spotlight who was a committed supporter of Breaking the Cycle.

When I went to see Morry, I was hoping he

would commit Spotlight to offering five jobs, so that I could then approach other employers and leverage off Morry's commitment until I had a dozen or so jobs, enough to justify a program. I was adamant that, if Spotlight were to employ our graduates, it had to be a business decision and not a gesture of charity. I had enough experience to know that the warm inner glow of charity soon fades if the employee fails to live up to expectations, and I said as much to Morry.

Somehow I convinced Morry of the value of the proposition. I knew I could guarantee that the young people he was to employ would be grateful for their opportunity, highly motivated, keen to learn, responsible in their behaviour and willing to listen to feedback and instructions. If they weren't, they wouldn't graduate from the program. And because they had all been unemployed for so long, they all came with an employment subsidy, so that by the time Spotlight had to pay out salaries, they would have a very clear sense of whether the young person was a worthwhile employee or not. It was a no-lose deal.

Based on our first two programs, I was extremely confident of our training ability. With the incentive of a job at the end, I knew the results would be even better.

Always one to drive a bargain, Morry asked, 'Who pays for the training?'

'You guarantee the jobs and I reckon I could get the government to pay for the training,' I replied.

'Good,' Morry said. 'I'll take 25 to start with.'

I nearly fell over. 'Er, right. I'll get back to you.'

I couldn't believe my ears. Here I was in my first meeting, being offered 25 jobs. Up until now, we had only had thirteen in a program. I had just agreed to effectively double our program capacity and get the government to pay for it.

Fortunately, I was able to set up a personal meeting with the Victorian director of the relevant government department. Our case was pretty simple. It was also a no-lose deal for the government. They would pay Breaking the Cycle to train 25 of the most challenged young people registered at the Commonwealth Employment Service, and we would guarantee to have them employed or we would pay the training fee back.

I also wanted to put pressure on labour market programs to lift their game across the board. At the time the national success rate for getting long-term unemployed people into jobs through other employment programs was 26 per cent. Organisations were being paid 100 per cent of their fees to deliver a 26 per cent result. What other industry would tolerate this as an acceptable success rate?

What transpired was a performance-based contract that grew to more than $2 million per year and catapulted us from an entrepreneurial start-up idea to a fully fledged non-profit business. In what can only be described as a 'Yes Ministerish' fashion, the government negotiated us down from an 85 per cent success rate to only 75 per cent. Their logic? That 85 per cent was ridiculously high, and would be unachievable. They drove a hard bargain, so we reluctantly agreed.

It was around this time that Jenny Navaro came on board full-time. Jenny had been a supporter raising funds in the background, and had an enormous amount of administrative experience. She had been the senior secretary to the head of the legal department at Western Mining. Jenny was able to negotiate going part-time at Western Mining so that she could put in half a day with us, setting up our administration systems and procedures. (I should add that half a day at Breaking the Cycle was twelve hours; there are 24 hours in a day, after all.) Jenny was a godsend, and before long she resigned from her job at Western Mining and became an integral part of Breaking the Cycle. She had the unenviable task of getting me organised. Piece of cake for a trained digger.

So we were away. With the assistance of the CES, we recruited 25 long-term unemployed young people and trained them into what became known as the 'Spotlight Youth Employment Scheme'. Because all the jobs were with Spotlight, we were able to tailor the program to meet the company's specific requirements. As part of the deal, each Spotlight store designated a person to act as a mentor on site to ensure a smooth transition into work.

The program was a spectacular success, and it became the template for how we conducted programs across Australia for the next five years. Logistically, the recruitment stage was a nightmare, but once the 25 or so young people were in their seats on day one, the rest was relatively easy.

The jobs were posted on every CES bulletin within range of a participating store. The CES would then send us three or four young people per job to attend an information session. The session would explicitly describe the program. We would explicitly tell the young people that, even if they hadn't worked for years or had never had a job, there were easier ways to get a job than doing this program. We would continue, 'If you are genuinely happy with the way your life is, then you are free to leave now. You've met your obligation to the CES, and there won't be any negative repercussions. But if there are aspects of your life you aren't happy with and you want to make some positive changes, stick around. This program is likely to be the best opportunity you'll get for a while.'

We made the program appear tough to get into and easy to get out of. Experience had taught me that unless young people are genuinely committed to getting their lives on track, the chances are that they won't be able to sustain the effort required to break out of the negative cycles that are holding them back. But people also need the opportunities; this was where having a pre-negotiated job was priceless.

The program was designed to give young people an opportunity to confront their demons, begin to heal the scars left by past experiences and move on, so that they had more control over how they conducted their lives. Limiting behaviours such as uncontrolled anger, frustration, resentments, depression or drug dependency often surface when people are placed under pressure. For many, the program was just the start of a long journey of recovery. The difference was that they knew recovery was not only possible but probable.

Many times, individuals would want to quit. No

doubt there were many times when it appeared all too hard. The pain, the loneliness, the feelings of not being understood or accepted became all too much. Being out in the wilderness only exacerbated the situation, which is why we were there.

On the third program, a young man I'll call Pete came very close to giving up. Pete had been abused and abandoned by his family from a very young age. By the time he was sixteen, he had lived in more than thirty foster homes. He had been physically and sexually abused in some of them, and when things got too close for comfort, he would shoot through. By the fourth day of the Spotlight program, the heat was on our young friend.

'That's it! I've had enough of this bullshit. I'm out of here,' was the cry from Pete's tent, almost on cue. Here we go, I thought; this will be interesting. 'What's up?' I asked. I won't repeat Pete's analysis of the program, Breaking the Cycle, Spotlight, me, my heritage and life in general. Suffice it to say that he was doing it hard.

But up to this point he had been doing really well. This was part of Pete's challenge. He was beginning to experience being accepted and valued, and he was very uncomfortable with the possibility of fitting in and getting close to people.

'I want to go home,' he said. 'You said I have a choice, and I choose to go home.' He was looking pretty pleased with himself. I knew that if I didn't agree with him, he would put me into the same basket as everyone else who had lied to him.

'You haven't got a home,' I replied. 'You're homeless. You tell me just exactly what it is you're going back to?' Provocatively, I continued, 'Isn't that one of the reasons your life is the way it is? Mate, there is nothing you can do to change what happened to you in the past and no argument it was lousy. If there was something I could do to change it I would, but I can't. What I can do is support you to make it better from now on. But that is up to you. You said you wanted your life be different, to have more choices, to have friends who expect more of you than you do of yourself. Well, this is it. You might want to quit on yourself because it is all too hard, but we won't quit on you.'

I gave him 30 minutes to think about it. I told him that if he really wanted his life to stay the way it was, then we'd make arrangements for him to go home. But I reminded him, 'There's a job at the end of this program with an employer who wants you. There's only one person in this conversation who can prevent you from starting, and it isn't me.' I suggested that Pete think about why he chose to come on the program and consider the big picture of how he wanted his life to be. 'I know you are up to it,' I said, 'and if you can handle this, then you are going to have more strength to handle some of the other stuff in your life. But if you give up, what's going to be different?'

With that I left him alone for half an hour. When the time was up, he told us he would give us one more chance. I thanked him for the opportunity. On graduation evening, I asked him how we went. The answer came amid tears and hugs.

Like 90 per cent of the 150 young people Spotlight employed over the next eighteen months, and with the support of his in-store mentor, Pete became and remained a valuable member of the Spotlight team.

*

Challenges present themselves in many and varied guises. At the end of the three-day canoe leg on the third program, there were some pretty tired and aching bodies, but the group was travelling reasonably well, apart from the usual challenges of having to dig a hole to go to the toilet or set up your tent in 20-knot winds. Our next leg was to be two and a half days of mountain-bike riding on bush tracks to our residential destination at Ontos.

On the morning of the fifth day, a very quiet young man whom I will call Steve approached me and told me he thought he might have to leave the group.

I was quite taken aback. I knew Steve was shy, but that was no reason to go home. I couldn't imagine what was so bad that he wanted to leave. Steve swore me to secrecy, and then confided that he couldn't ride a bike. Bloody hell! I hadn't thought to ask. We knew everyone's swimming levels, any debilitating illnesses or injuries, but we hadn't asked if they could ride bikes. Steve was quite embarrassed about his predicament; he had just never learnt to ride. Simple as that.

The ride was designed to stretch even some of the more experienced riders. It was mostly uphill, and there were sections where everyone had to dismount and carry their bikes across creeks or over logs.

I gathered the team together for the morning briefing and after the designated leaders had run through the outline of the day, with Steve's permission I told them about his problem. I suggested that we would need some input from everyone, because if we weren't able to achieve our goal as a team because one of us lacked the appropriate training, then that would impact on all of us. 'Then let's train him,' said one of the team. 'Let's teach him how to ride a bike.'

The next two and a half days were amazing. This was not like learning to ride a bike at the age of four or five, with Mum or Dad running alongside encouraging your little legs to 'pedal, pedal, pedal'. There was none of the security of using training wheels on a concrete drive.

Inadvertently, Steve provided a fantastic opportunity for us all to gain direct experience of everything we had been speaking about conceptually. We all got to see the value of practical support, encouragement, feedback, correcting and learning from mistakes. Steve and the team embraced the task in a good spirit; it was a practical demonstration that together, everyone achieves more.

After many, many wobbly falls, Steve began to master this new and complex task. It was unlikely he was ever going to wear the yellow jersey on the Tour de France, but he was having a red-hot go, having to deal with fears. Steve was experiencing what it felt like to overcome a major physical and mental challenge.

He had got over his initial embarrassment, and he also overcame his initial belief that he couldn't ride a bike. Within a few hours he was riding, if very cautiously along some very difficult and demanding tracks.

The next scene, I swear, I will take to my grave. On the last section of the bike leg, all the team except Steve and his two designated 'minders' had reached the destination for the evening. Instead of the usual routine – dismount, park the bikes and set up camp – the team waited in silence for Steve and his buddies to arrive. The team split in two, forming a guard of honour on both sides of the track.

As Steve rode through, they all cheered, hollered and threw their helmets in the air in recognition of this young man's achievement. There were only a few dry eyes. It was yet another demonstration of the power of young people when given the chance to show their true colours.

As a postscript, that young man, who entered the program painfully shy, unable to hold a coherent conversation with his peers, let alone an adult in authority, is now heading up a department at Spotlight and proved to be an outstanding mentor for other graduates.

After six days of residential life skills at Ontos, we returned to Melbourne, where we set up a mock Spotlight Store in our training room. We had cash registers, haberdashery boards and fabric cutting all on site. Spotlight staff delivered this part of the training. By the end, Sandra Duggan, who had been appointed Spotlight's co-coordinator of the program, wasn't sure whether she was working for Spotlight or Breaking the Cycle. She worked tirelessly to ensure the program would succeed.

And succeed it did, by every measure. The young graduates were placed in stores right across metropolitan Melbourne. Morry was very happy with the result, and before long accepted my invitation to join the Board of Breaking the Cycle. I suggested if he wanted us to train young people and mentors for all his stores across Australia, he had better get in early, as positions were filling fast.

9
Going National

After the publicity surrounding the success of the Spotlight program, Breaking the Cycle was in hot demand. Within a couple of months we were getting an enquiry a week from people from all over Australia asking if we would set up Breaking the Cycle in their communities. We even had enquiries from America and Canada. My response was always the same. We are busy, but if you are prepared to do what we do then I'm more than willing to help you. But when most people realised how much commitment, effort and energy was required, they didn't ring back. To set up a new program required hundreds of hours of preparation and training, not to mention the job commitments from local employers.

The first three years at Breaking the Cycle were exciting to be part of. There was a real air of magic about the place. It seemed anything was possible, and if it wasn't possible then it wasn't meant to happen. We were very fortunate in the people we attracted to work in the organisation. We had quite a few young people working for us, graduates of the program and others, who were amazing role models for those coming through.

One such young man was Matt Scarf. Matt hailed from Bendigo, the regional city in north-central Victoria, and had been a leader at Discovery, the organisation Terry Molloy had facilitated. Matt was one of those young men who looked anywhere between 18 and 25. All the girls thought he was gorgeous, which didn't hurt either. He had a strong sense of integrity and would not compromise his standards under any circumstances. This at times set him on a collision course with others within the organisation, including Terry. But Matt would stick to his guns. This often annoyed the hell out of Terry, and provided me with some interesting management challenges.

Matt eventually left the organisation on the best of terms and moved to Byron Bay, where he set up a surf school. About twelve months later, I took a holiday at Byron Bay with Sharon and our son Jordan, and we caught up with Matt. His surf school was doing well. He was surfing every day, mainly teaching backpackers from all around the world, and he had a beautiful Scandinavian girlfriend. My fleeting fantasy of luring him back to Melbourne to earn less money working for Breaking the Cycle remained just that.

What made the difference at Breaking the Cycle was the extraordinary love and respect people had for each other. People wanted to work there because of the way they were treated. Not that we didn't have our differences of opinions, styles and personalities, but we had an overriding commitment to resolving conflict in a way that worked for everyone. A 'do whatever it takes' attitude prevailed, and everyone gave above and beyond the call of duty. This environment attracted many people because it embodied the principles we were introducing young people to. We weren't without mistakes, but there was a genuine commitment to learn from those mistakes.

It seemed almost every week there was an article about Breaking the Cycle in a newspaper or magazine. *TIME* magazine did an article on us, ***BUSINESS REVIEW WEEKLY*** congratulated us on our radical new approach to engaging corporate Australia, and I was frequently asked to comment on issues pertaining to unemployed kids. It was a great help that we had two prominent national patrons: Max Walker, former Australian cricketer and TV personality, and Karen Knowles, singer and international recording artist. The morning TV programs were very happy to talk to me as long as Karen sang for them.

In 1994 I received a Community Service Award from the Committee for Melbourne. It was odd to be standing in the obligatory penguin suit alongside the legendary AFL coach Kevin Sheedy and the Chilean Ambassador, who were also recipients. There was a real feeling that Breaking the Cycle was making some real headway towards re-engaging the thousands of young people who found themselves excluded from mainstream society.

As I said earlier, only a few of those who had requested our help rang back, but there were some wonderful people among those who did. Maryanne Lewis was working with a community group in Ballarat, about an hour's drive west of Melbourne. I had a soft spot for Ballarat; I remembered playing football there in the snow in my younger days. After a couple of meetings it became clear that Maryanne had the tenacity required to succeed in this caper, so we began the process of setting up our first regional office. In hindsight it was probably was a little too soon, and our meagre resources were somewhat stretched. Maryanne went about inspiring and cajoling people to help her set up an office and employ her to manage the project. Sharon and I relocated to Ballarat for three months to assist in enrolling the community and getting the all-important jobs. The level of community support was terrific. The local paper and radio station got behind us, and Breaking the Cycle became the talk of the town.

At the time the Premier of Victoria, Jeff Kennett, had sacked all the State's democratically elected local government councillors and replaced them with government-appointed commissioners. It is not for me to comment on the broader political ramifications of Mr Kennett's decision, but it occurred to me that it could be easier talking to one Commissioner than lobbying up to a dozen councillors with factional commitments I didn't understand. Who said totalitarianism is all bad? A meeting was set up with Ballarat's Chief Commissioner. He was sympathetic to our plight, but said it would be impossible for the Council to employ any young people in the current industrial climate, (the Council was in the process of retrenching staff and outsourcing services).

Sensing where this conversation was heading, I said, 'With respect, sir, we don't need your sympathy. We need your leadership. We need the City of Ballarat to get behind this effort and encourage others to do the same. This is not my community and they are not my kids, but if I were in your situation I wouldn't let this opportunity pass you by. We have been invited here because some key people in your city believe we have got something of value to offer.'

Maryanne gave me a panic-stricken look. I guess she was wondering whether she would ever get a job in Ballarat again. Then the Commissioner said, 'Well, as I said, we can't offer any jobs – the unions would savage us. How much does it cost to employ one of these young people for a year?'

'About $10,000 after employment subsidies.'

'Right. Then I will give five non-profit organisations $10,000 each so they can employ them. Will that do you?'

I knew that would be enough to get the ball rolling. I also asked the Commissioner if he would mind hosting a breakfast for employers so we could secure the other twenty positions we needed. 'Sure, love to,' he said.

With that, Breaking the Cycle was off and racing in Ballarat. I looked across and winked at Maryanne, who had gone a little quiet.

Within a month there was a business breakfast hosted by the City of Ballarat. Max Walker had agreed to be the MC and to entertain the guests over their bacon and eggs. The big bloke is a national icon and must be one of the most popular people in Australia. When I travelled with Max to Sydney and Brisbane to promote Breaking the Cycle, you had to set aside at least an extra hour to accommodate all the people who wanted to have a yarn with him.

The Ballarat breakfast was due to start at 7.30am at the famous Craig's Hotel. We all stayed at the hotel the night before. Max spent the evening as a guest speaker on a panel at a celebrity sportsmen's night to raise funds for St Patrick's College in Ballarat. Now, I don't recall getting to bed before ten, and I sure didn't hear Max come in. Just after 7am, I decided I had better give the big bloke a courtesy call. I called, I knocked and knocked, and just when I thought it would be a good time to panic, out came the former fast bowler, and I have got to tell you he was not looking good.

'You all right, big fella?' I enquired. A meek grin from behind the teeth was the reply.

I know that grin, I thought. This should be interesting. I was sure the fifty or so people at the breakfast hadn't got up early and paid $25 to listen to me go on about why they should employ a Breaking the Cycle graduate.

But a miraculous transformation occurred between the bottom of the stairs and the entrance to the dining room where our guests awaited the big man. Max was absolutely sensational from the moment he entered the room. Engaging, personable, powerful, animated, passionate and very, very funny. In no time, he had the audience eating out of his hand. He worked the room and shared the profound personal experiences he had had with our graduates. By the time he had finished, signing up employers was a formality. They formed an orderly queue in order for us to get their details.

Breaking the Cycle was in Ballarat for almost two years and found jobs for about 120 young people who most likely would never have had a chance otherwise. And, more importantly, it enabled all of them to experience far more of who they were.

*

Around this time, I received a phone call from a woman in Brisbane. 'Hi, my name is Priscilla McNamara and I am a friend of Terry Molloy. Tezza tells me you are expanding Breaking the Cycle, and I was wondering if you could help me expand the program I facilitate with unemployed people in Brisbane?

I thought, bloody hell, I'm not sure how I am going to expand Breaking the Cycle. How on earth am I going to help you? 'I'll tell you what I'll do,' I said. 'Give me half an hour to tell you what we are doing, and if in half an hour you reckon what you are doing is better than what we are doing, I will do what I can to help you. If on the other hand if you think what we are doing is better than your program, then I want your help to set up Breaking the Cycle in Queensland. Fair enough?'

The deal was struck, and three hours later Priscilla had agreed to get on a plane at her own expense and spend six weeks with me and the rest of the organisation, with a view to going back to Queensland and being our State Manager.

Priscilla threw herself in lock, stock and barrel. She shadowed and understudied every key person in the organisation. She volunteered on programs, learnt our administrative systems and procedures, and soaked herself in our culture. It was a crash course in everything to do with Breaking the Cycle.

When she returned to Brisbane, Priscilla took responsibility for what would become the most successful division of the organisation. Sharon and I once more relocated for three months to assist with the establishment phase. This time it was a good deal warmer, and our baby son,

Jordan, didn't seem to mind where we were.

Priscilla was a fantastic networker. She enrolled a 'Who's Who' of Brisbane, including the State government, the business community and the Brisbane Broncos. In its four or five years of operation, Queensland Breaking the Cycle was able to do every bit as well as us in Victoria, and sometimes better, thanks to the dedication and commitment of Priscilla and her small team. It was no surprise when she received a Telstra Businesswoman of the Year award. She thoroughly deserved it. In her home in East Brisbane is a beautiful photo of Priscilla with the Dalai Lama. At a birthday party in her honour, I once remarked that more than one person had looked at the photograph with love and respect and asked, 'Who is that bloke with Priscilla?'

In the early days of setting up the Brisbane office, a graduate of the second Breaking the Cycle program waltzed in unannounced. Chrissy was a young Aboriginal woman who was about twenty years old when she was referred to me from the Open Family Foundation. The Open Family works with the most alienated street people, the young people most organisations do not want to know about. At the time, Chrissy was no exception. She was a large young woman living in a doss house in the inner city; she had a drinking habit, no money, no apparent future and no hope.

Chrissy had come down from the country, where she had been brought up by a loving white family who had adopted her at a very early age. She had no idea of who her biological parents were, and felt caught between two worlds. To the whites she was black and to the blacks she was a 'coconut', brown on the outside and white on the inside. She felt displaced, with no sense of identity or belonging, despite her adopted family's best effort and intentions.

Chrissy's lifestyle was typical of that of many long-term unemployed and homeless young people. She wasn't just homeless; she was without a sense of a constructive community. Her chances of being successful in keeping a job at this stage of her life were remote. There were a few significant challenges to overcome first. So, rather than set her up to fail, we began supporting her to handle some of her problems.

The first task was to get her into stable, safe and secure accommodation. We rented a house directly across the road from where Sharon and I were living, and gave Chrissy the responsibility of keeping the place drug and alcohol-free. That way we could accommodate three or four other young participants who also needed a 'clean space' to live in.

Chrissy wasn't 100 per cent successful with that responsibility, but it was a hundred times better than the previous few years. She began to have a sense of order and 'normality' in her life. The next step was to connect Chrissy with her passion, her spirit. We discovered that she was a talented artist, so I commissioned several paintings and paid her a deposit so she could buy the materials. The down-payment also helped to ensure she would complete the job.

The artwork she produced was excellent. One of her paintings now hangs in a gallery in San Francisco as part of a cultural exchange. Far more than producing great art, painting put

Chrissy in touch with her aboriginality. Until then, she had been living from dole cheque to dole cheque with no sense of purpose or self-worth. It was a privilege to witness the emergence of this powerful young woman.

Chrissy still had no idea of her biological parents and why she was 'given up' for adoption. For the first few months that I knew her, she was very reluctant to discuss her background. When the matter was raised, she would often shrug her shoulders and say, 'Who cares?'

'Good question,' I would reply.

It was obvious she cared deeply, but in order to trace her family she had to confront all of her 'what if' questions. What if it didn't work out? Could she cope with further rejection and heartache? To begin to find her family, she had to make a serious commitment to herself, so that she wouldn't quit on herself, no matter what the outcome of her discovery. She had been denying her need to connect with her family, her culture, her 'mob', because she had not felt strong enough to overcome her fears.

With the appropriate support, encouragement and time, Chrissy took the first step, calling an agency that specialised in reuniting adopted children with their biological families. Her search took more than two years and extended across three States. Her patience was an important lesson for me; I'm the sort of person who wants everything done yesterday.

So here we were in Brisbane when Chrissy walked in out of the blue. 'Hi,' she said. 'Just got into town, thought I'd say g'day.'

I hadn't seen her for some time, and she had no idea I was in Brisbane. It was a case of very good timing. I soon established that she had nowhere to stay and had only $30 to keep her going until her dole payment. Without hesitation I suggested Chrissy come and stay with Sharon and me for a couple of weeks in exchange for doing some housework and occasionally minding our little son.

As luck would have it, Karen Knowles was also staying with us for a couple of days. Karen has always had a keen interest in issues affecting Aboriginal people, and she knew Tiger Bayles, the manager of the Brisbane-based aboriginal radio station, 4AAA. With one phone call, Karen arranged for us to meet Tiger at the radio station.

After we had spoken for a little while, Tiger strolled into the 'on air' studio and asked the presenter if he could take over his program for ten minutes. 'Sure, brother,' the presenter said. Before we knew it, Chrissy, Karen and I were doing an impromptu live-to-air interview.

Tiger began by introducing Karen and her connection with Breaking the Cycle and then got me talking about Breaking the Cycle and our plans in Queensland. He then introduced Chrissy as a graduate of Breaking the Cycle, and a young local girl looking for her mob. Tiger asked Chrissy what she knew of her mother, and appealed to anyone out there listening to ring in if they had any further information that might help reunite Chrissy with her family.

The response was amazing. Within five minutes there were four separate calls providing pinpoint information about Chrissy's mother and extended family. Chrissy was in shock. For the first time in her life, she had hard evidence about her family and where she had come from.

The phone calls continued for days, and soon Chrissy was speaking with people who knew her mother and a sister she didn't know she had.

Tiger then arranged for Chrissy to live with his mother. For the first time in her life she truly felt she belonged. She lived with Tiger's mum for three years.

Today Chrissy is the proud mother of a beautiful little girl, and has really connected with her culture. She sees her sister regularly, though she has been unable to meet up with her mother. Chrissy knows it is a matter of timing, and that her mother must have her own reasons for not wanting to meet her yet. Once again I stand in awe of a young person who had the courage to commit herself to taking responsibility for her own life.

*

Despite a great deal of time and effort, we were never able to establish a solid foothold in Sydney. We had some terrific program results, but we were never able to settle the way we had in Ballarat and Brisbane. Maybe it was a Sydney-Melbourne thing, but I suspect it was mainly that we weren't able to unearth a Maryanne Lewis or Pricilla McNamara.

Almost from our inception, a couple of committed people from Albury had urged us to set up a regional office in their community. Paul Hibbard had been working his backside off for years to create effective services for the young people of his district. Hibbo was an amazing man – quiet, unassuming yet extraordinarily persuasive. His right-hand man was Gabe Farrow, a local businessman whose family was well respected in the Albury/Wodonga region.

As well as being extraordinarily successful and a committed family man, Gabe was the owner of Better Loosen Up, the only Australian racehorse to ever win a Japan Cup, which carried prize money of $4 million. Gabe said to me one day, 'You know, Paul, people think because you win the Japan Cup you have got lots of money. No one appreciates the expenses involved. Do you know how expensive it was to buy the suitcases to bring all that money home?'

Gabe was extremely generous and was struck by Hibbo's passionate commitment to the disaffected youth of society. They were a formidable pair, and it was only a matter of time before Breaking the Cycle was running programs in partnership with their Albury/Wodonga Youth Projects.

Sadly, Hibbo and Gabe passed away within six months of each other. They were good men and we are all the poorer for their passing. Hibbo was 41 and suffered a heart attack. I had lunch with him only hours before he died. He had driven down from Albury, and over lunch he reaffirmed his support for what we were doing at Breaking the Cycle. As we parted, the big bear of a man gave me a massive hug, and we went our separate ways with tears in our eyes. I remember distinctly thinking how lucky I was to have men like Hibbo in my life. The next morning I got a call to tell me Paul had suffered a massive heart attack and died. I was flattened.

*

In seven years of operation, Breaking the Cycle had over 1200 young people graduate from its programs. Young people came from every State and territory in Australia, and 97 per cent of those who started a program successfully graduated into a pre-negotiated job. Six months later, 85 per cent were still gainfully employed, and I believe the other 15 per cent learnt just as much. All of this was achieved through the commitment, passion and dedication of hundreds of people across Australia.

So what happened?

10
Success Was Not Enough

I could have been forgiven for thinking that Breaking the Cycle had a bright future when the Howard government restructured the labour market and privatised the system of support for unemployed people. One would think so. It was not as if our job was complete. The government had decided to undertake the greatest reform in labour market services since World War Two. In the upshot, in spite of our extraordinary results, Breaking the Cycle failed to secure a contract under the new system. And, unfortunately for us, the government was our only paying customer.

Since 1992 we had been building the organisation, doing more and more programs each year. We had never tendered for our contract; we had just approached the government with a model that worked and a bunch of national employers who wanted to employ long-term unemployed young people as long as they had been through a Breaking the Cycle program. Pretty simple, but the effect was to make us dependent on the government for our cash flow.

After the Howard government won the 1998 election, it announced it was going to get rid of the Commonwealth Employment Service and introduce a new privatised system that would provide job seekers with a choice of services to assist them in finding work. In hindsight, I don't believe any of us really appreciated the significance of the government's announced changes. The government was extremely sensitive to being accused of playing favourites, so it set up a tendering process and appointed an external auditing company to process the tenders. It probably had to be done that way, but the company concerned had very little understanding of the labour market environment, and our track record counted for nought.

Regardless of whether we were successful in securing a contract in the new system, we knew it was the end of an era for Breaking the Cycle. We weren't sure how the new system would affect our ability to run programs for the young people who needed them the most. I was concerned, but not about what would happen if we failed to get a contract. I was more worried about what would happen if we did. You see, Breaking the Cycle was not just a labour market service provider whose sole purpose was to place people in jobs. We had a much larger agenda. We were about giving young people the chance to turn their lives around, to begin to appreciate their true worth and move their lives in a positive direction. I wasn't convinced we could do that competitively under the new system. As it turned out, I didn't have to worry about that.

The announcement came. Breaking the Cycle, along with 300 other services of the 600 that applied, failed to secure a contract. The announcement was almost surreal. I don't know whether we were arrogant, but after providing the government with better than 85% employment outcomes across Australia year in, year out, I honestly thought the government couldn't be so stupid as to reject our application. But there was another part of me that always knew we wouldn't get a contract; to this day, I am unable to put my finger on what made me think that.

There was a fair bit of shock around the place, and a fair bit of righteous indignation as well. How dare they not give Breaking the Cycle a contract? The truth was that we were utterly insignificant in the government's scheme of things, and our only real mistake had been to think otherwise. Breaking the Cycle did not rate a blip on the radar.

Before the 1996 election, the shadow minister for Employment and Youth Affairs, Dr David Kemp, had visited Breaking the Cycle and met twenty or so young people who were in the last week of a program. Dr Kemp and I sat at the front of the room as I introduced him. I said, 'If the Liberal party wins government, this man is going to be very important in deciding what labour market programs get funding from the government and which ones don't. You guys all have signed an agreement to tell the truth about what you are thinking and how you are feeling. All I ask is that you tell the truth. You don't have to exaggerate – the truth is enough.'

What transpired over the next hour or so was profoundly moving Each young person spoke openly and honestly about their lives and their experience over the past few weeks. More than half the group admitted they had seriously considered taking their own lives, and about half a dozen of them had actually attempted suicide. Yet here they were sharing their hopes and ambitions for the future, talking about what they had learnt and how they were going to use their learning in less than a week in their new jobs.

Some were in tears as they shared their stories, and Dr Kemp was visibly moved by the experience. On his way out, he turned to me and asked, 'How long would it take to roll Breaking the Cycle out across Australia?' 'Three years,' I replied. But I suppose it wasn't to be.

My gripe is that the young people who most require assistance are being more let down by the new system more than ever before. A large number of young people like those we took on our programs are not even making it into the system in the first place because of their transient and chaotic lifestyles.

For those young people that do make it into the system, the government now outsources the provision of services to organisations on a fee-for-service basis. The only problem is that the people who require the most intensive assistance by and large don't get it. There are two reasons for this. First, it is expensive and cuts into the organisation's profit; and secondly, most organisations do not have the experience or program methodology to facilitate the necessary changes. If they did, an employment outcome of 85 per cent would not be so remarkable.

Remember the old success rate of 26 per cent? It hasn't got any better; in fact, I know of one organisation that at the time of writing had a 6 per cent success rate with the same sort of young people we enrolled. It may sound like sour grapes, but it is far beyond that for me. It is a national disgrace that the knowledge and experience gained by Breaking the Cycle was lost to the community.

*

Within a year, Breaking the Cycle went from being a vibrant, exciting, leading-edge organisation to one that imploded and went out of business. The pressure we experienced was unbearable.

On Friday, 7 August 1998, John Tripodi went home from work, had the traditional fish and chips with his two young sons, put them to bed and had a fatal heart attack. He was twelve days short of his 41st birthday.

Our phone rang on Saturday morning at 7.30am and Sharon answered it. I didn't think much of it until I heard her burst into tears from the other side of the house.

'John is dead' she said.

'John who?'

'John Tripodi.'

I sat down in a state of shock. 'That can't be right. Who was that on the phone?' I said, as if hoping the person was not qualified to know. I guess denial is a pretty typical response to such confronting news. I rang Richard Keddie, a really close buddy of John's. If anyone knew, Rich would. Rich had been with John when he died. John had felt a heart attack coming on and called Rich, who lived just around the corner. Rich was there in minutes and called an ambulance on his way around. John died in Richards's arms before the ambulance arrived.

I find it difficult to express how I felt. Shocked, numb, incredibly sad. I feel a part of me died with him. John was such a huge personality; the hole he left was commensurate. In the years since then, there isn't a day goes by when I don't remember my mate Troppo. To say he was a good man is to sell him short. I miss him.

John's death kicked the stuffing out of us. He left a huge hole in the organisation. In hindsight, Breaking the Cycle never had a chance to survive once we failed to secure a contract within the new job network, but none of us wanted to hear that. Least of all me.

This was the toughest period of my life. I was sad, I was mad, and I was at a loss about what to do. Grieving for my buddies, pissed off with the government for its short-sightedness and spinelessness, I was fighting for the survival of the thing that gave me a sense of purpose in my life.

The future looked grim. By this time almost all of our remaining staff had gone nearly five months without pay. Many of them had taken part-time jobs and were coming in on their own time to do what they could to help.

Vic and I went to see quite a few of our past benefactors and supporters to ask for assistance to keep Breaking the Cycle afloat. Among them was Geoff Harris of Flight Centre, the highly successful budget travel company Geoff had created in the early 1980s. Having heard our plight, Geoff contacted me and asked me to gather our remaining staff together for a meeting at 2pm the following Wednesday.

The hour arrived and so did Geoff's wife, Sue. We had about six staff left at this stage. Geoff spoke, acknowledging everyone's dedication and great work. He then reached into his top pocket and presented me with a personal cheque made out to Breaking the Cycle for $50,000. He said, 'Paul, I hope this goes some way to keeping your vision alive.' We were all a bit stunned as well as pleased.

After all the staff had left the room, I spoke to Geoff and Sue. I told them that things weren't looking too good. Even with their extremely generous gift, there was no guarantee we could save the organisation. Geoff turned to me and said, 'Pay your people, Paul. There are no strings attached.'

11
One Door Closes

'One door closes, another one opens.' I wish it were as easy as that. Formally Breaking the Cycle went into voluntary administration in December 1999. That was a bit of a misnomer. There wasn't much volunteering on my part. Day by day people were leaving and finding themselves new jobs. It was a sad moment when I finally turned the lights out. By then, there was just me and the goldfish.

For the first time in my life, I was at a dead set loss about what to do. I had to earn a living, yet there was nothing that appealed to me, or that I had the energy for. I needed a break to rest and recover but the more time I spent doing nothing, the more disturbed and restless I became.

Sharon had secured a contract with a Statewide organisation, so I decided I would stay at home with our two children. Our second son, David, was now around two years old, and I thought I would spend some quality time with both the boys, a rare and previously unforeseen opportunity. Sharon had most of our running costs covered, so that was it. Mr Mum it was. I had visions of growing vegetables, baking bread, having time to do all those things I had been missing for years, like playing my guitar. Bugger it, I might do my Masters or get a PhD. Wrong again. It was bloody difficult. I soon found out why men are so keen to go to work and how demoralising it is when you don't or can't work.

For years I had been highly energetic, a driving force capable of inspiring others to confront their demons. Right now I was confronting mine, and I couldn't even get a two-year-old to finish his dinner.

Although I was surrounded by good people who I knew loved me, I felt as lonely as a bastard on father's day. I was depressed, though I didn't realise it. I had very little energy. I couldn't be bothered doing anything other than the bare minimum to get through each day. I did not emerge as the 'earth father'; I hated my life and resented what had happened and who I had become.

I knew that for things to change, first I must, but where could I start? I was experiencing the same problems as so many of the young people I had counselled. So what would I advise them to do? 'Do something, anything. Action beats inaction. The worst that can happen is you will learn something.' All good advice, but easier said than done.

I did do something. I found a counsellor and began looking at my demons, my challenges, my emotions, my feelings, my disappointments, my perceived failures and inadequacies. I had spent so long assisting others I had lost touch with myself. So began the return journey, and I won't pretend it was the express route.

I had a bit of baggage to sort through. I had accumulated a lot of suppressed frustrations, disappointments and downright bloody annoyance at the unnecessary pain so many people live with daily. I had refused to let myself show any sign of 'weakness' or 'not coping'; I was the founder of

Breaking the Cycle, and if I started to lose it then the ramifications would have been catastrophic. As a result, I had spent a great deal of time and energy denying my feelings, holding it all in and becoming more and more unable to deal with the challenges I had in my life.

Being sufficiently present with oneself to know what is truly going on is, in my experience, fairly rare. Particularly for men. It is far easier to get busy, too busy to be in touch with your feelings. I hear plenty of men say, 'I haven't got time for this stuff. Besides, who cares anyway? What difference is it going to make?' Plenty, I say. For a start, being in touch with your feelings and expressing them may not change the external situation, but it does reduce your frustration and anger. Many men and young boys do not know how to express their feelings in a healthy way. It took the demise of Breaking the Cycle for me to begin to do so, and I am still learning. You see, I had confused achieving success with being happy.

A good friend of mine, Dave Austin, spent all his waking hours building successful businesses only to discover there are an awful lot of 'successful cripples' out there. People who have achieved enormous success in their lives only to realise they didn't know who they truly were or what made them happy. Dave sold up and retired in his early forties – his goal since he was a young man. He was now confronted with himself, his feelings, his emotions and the truth. To his credit, Dave didn't throw himself into another project to distract him from himself; he took the more challenging road of getting to know himself intimately. I have learnt a great deal from Dave. His friendship and uncompromising support played a key role in my regaining my happiness and purpose in life.

*

Fortunately I had an opportunity to develop a Breaking the Cycle-type program for young people with intellectual disabilities in Wollongong. This turned out to be a blessing, as I needed to do something useful to keep me active and help pay the bills.

About eight months before Breaking the Cycle closed, I received a phone call from a woman called Judy Augustyn who managed a disability service in NSW. 'Do you think what you do could work with the people I work with?' she asked.

I thought for a moment, and the words of the Dalai Lama came to me. When once asked a profound question about the meaning of life, he said, 'I don't know.' This was my response to Judy. (If it was good enough for the Dalai Lama it was good enough for me.)

I had never worked with people with intellectual disabilities before, and I knew very little about them. I said I would come to Wollongong for two days and meet some young people who would be typical of those Judy would want to do a program, and also I would spend a day with her staff. Before I left, I would tell Judy whether or not I reckoned we could design a program to suit their needs.

The arrangements were made. I was met by one of the Illawarra Workwise staff at Sydney Airport and enjoyed a pleasant drive south to the coastal city of Wollongong.

I met half a dozen young people, and within fifteen minutes I realised they were going to be no bother. They were just doing human like the rest of us. It was the staff I was most concerned about. My experience is that people working in the welfare sector tend to be a little protective and defensive about their work. That is probably because they cop a fair bit of flak. but I also believe it is because they know deep down what they are doing is not effective enough.

But, to their credit, the staff at Illawarra Workwise admitted they were dissatisfied with their results over the past two years or so. They couldn't attract enough young people, they struggled to find jobs for those they had, and they felt they were not able to provide the services the young people needed in order to survive in open employment.

Right, then. Better get to work. No time like the present. So began the creation of what has developed into the most successful program of its kind for young people with intellectual disabilities and other impairments in Australia today.

I started with the staff. You can't expect to teach other people what you don't know or can't demonstrate by example. During several visits over six months or so, I took the staff team through a similar process to what we were about to do with their young people.

I taught them how to attract employers to commit jobs up-front from a business mentality, not out of charity. I held information sessions for young people and their families to introduce them to the concept of believing they were capable of learning what was required to succeed in the workplace, and I trained the staff in the frameworks of a re-badged and expanded Breaking the Cycle program, now known as Challenging the Future. The idea was not to simplify the program content, but to pace the young people into the process more gradually.

The program was divided into six modules, and was cleverly designed by the Workwise team to enable the young people to reach their level of ability and re-enter the program at a later stage without having to start at the beginning. This co-creation combined my experience with that of the Illawarra Workwise staff, whose background in the specialised area of intellectual disability was invaluable. As well as sharing my expertise, I got to learn an enormous amount myself.

It is worth describing the six modules in some detail. The first is Personal Preparation, which has young people taking part in the Duke of Edinburgh Award Scheme. The Duke of Edinburgh Award is open to any person aged between 14 and 25 looking for challenge, adventure and personal development. It presents young people with a clear range of challenges in the areas of skills, physical recreation, community service and expeditions, allowing participants to demonstrate their commitment to the program and learn about teamwork, planning and self-discipline. This module gives young people the opportunity to demonstrate their commitment to entering the workforce as well as improving communication, planning skills and initiative.

Module Two is about Vocational Preparation, getting familiar with the workplace. This module involves participation in work experiences in different employment settings. Exposure to real work environments allows young people to observe and model the qualities employers are looking for, and the variation in workplaces allows participants to make an informed choice about their future career. Illawarra Workwise staff accompany the young people on placements to train them in skills that can only be learnt in the workplace, such as teamwork, priority setting and communicating with customers and co-workers.

Module Three is about Job Selection, and introduces the motivation that creates committed, confident future employees. A number of participants complete a work trial for an employer who has committed a job. The employer, with assistance from Workwise, selects the most suitable candidate. This job helps to motivate the young people to complete the challenging training to come. The work trial positions offer further opportunities for training. The trials encourage young people to gain a clearer picture of the unique requirements of their future workplace. They experience situations they can refer to and work with during the rest of the program.

Only young people who complete the first three modules and are capable of succeeding in open employment can go on into Module Four. Those who don't immediately go on can do so later if they have demonstrated the necessary commitment to work. Young people often get caught up in the fantasy of going to work, and they will usually experience some pressure from family and friends. Then, when they actually check it out, some find that being employed is not all it is cracked up to be. Others are not ready to take the next step for one reason or another. That's OK; they are still supported in their journey towards what they are able to achieve.

Module Four is the wilderness trek and a work skills component, largely based on the Breaking the Cycle model. The young people take part in a three-week training program to teach them the key skills, abilities and behaviours that are a part of any successful workplace. The three-week program is divided into three sections: Life Skills, Wilderness Experience and Work Skills.

Life Skills is five days of accelerated learning in a course-room setting, designed to introduce concepts useful for future employment such as responsibility, teamwork, initiative and giving and receiving feedback. In the Wilderness Experience, the young people undertake a five-day journey in the bush. As with the Breaking the Cycle program, the time in the wilderness encourages the young people to practise concepts from the Life Skills week in an unfamiliar environment. The Work Skills week sees the young people return to the course-room setting to reflect on their increased range of skills and plan how to use them in the workplace.

An integral part of the third week is Mentor Day, when a mentor, nominated by the employer, participates in one day of the training. This provides an excellent opportunity for role modelling for the new worker. Consistent feedback has shown the mentor relationship to be an effective method of accelerated learning on the job. The mentors also receive training in leadership and communication skills, adding value to their organisation.

The three weeks are capped off with a graduation ceremony. On graduation night, the graduates receive a record of achievement and present a speech to the assembled family, friends, employers, mentors and community members. The ceremony celebrates the young person's movement into the workforce.

Module Five presents young people with the chance to demonstrate their training in their new workplace. After graduating, they begin work with guidance from their mentor and support from an Illawarra staff member. The jobs are part-time, so the employees can commit to work as well as participate in Module Six concurrently. Illawarra Workwise provides an on site staff member who assists in the transition into the workplace. At first, the staff member is constantly with the young person. This support is reduced as the young person settles into the position. This provides the employer with both an employee and a support person at no cost.

Recognising the value of positive peer support, we invite graduates of Challenging the Future to meet once a week in a 'Graduate Club', providing ongoing support. This is Module Six, which completes the process.

Challenging the Future is a comprehensive model that enables young people who have been assessed as being intellectually disabled to work in open employment, as opposed to a work enclave or a business unit, where they do repetitive piecework – what used to be called sheltered workshops.

I had been developing the life skills component of the program with my colleague Bob Curson-

Siggers, who had been the lead facilitator for Breaking the Cycle for the past three years. Bob is a brilliant communicator and has the perfect personality to succeed in this business. He is a 5th Dan Status karate expert and had been the head of his own karate organisation for ten years. Bob is as gentle as a lamb, but he can look seriously scary, which can be a real asset when you are putting full-on young people through their paces. Bob and I used to joke that for a couple of years we spent more nights together on programs across Australia than we did with our wives. I don't think our wives thought that was funny.

Anyhow, I wasn't going to do this Challenging the Future program without Bob. He kept asking me, 'What are they like, the young people? Can they read? Are they going to be able to comprehend what we are on about? What are they like?'

'No more or less than anyone else we had on our programs, I reckon,' was my reply.

In fact, working with the Challenging the Future participants is a good deal easier than working with long-term unemployed and alienated young people. But we did not know that then.

The big day arrived. For five months, Illawarra Workwise had been preparing the young people for the Bobby and Paul Show, more formally referred to as Module Four of Challenging the Future. Bob was to facilitate the program from the front of the room, while I stayed at the back to make sure the logistics were working. Before we started the formal training, I went to the front of the room and asked the group, 'Can

I have a show of hands? All those people who have been told they have a learning difficulty. Notice my hand is up. You ask my year 9 maths teacher and he would tell you I had a learning difficulty. OK now, who has been told they have an intellectual disability? Hands up! Let me see. Compared with what? Lets say compared to a rocket scientist, I have an intellectual disability. But who said it is a competition?'

I then asked them a couple more questions. 'Who walked in the room this morning? Everyone, good. How did you learn to do that? Walking on two legs is a very complex task. How do you learn to do it? How many of you can speak English? All of you? Great, how did you learn that? English is a very complex language, yet everyone in this room can speak it. Interesting. Can anyone speak any other languages? A couple of you? Great. I can't. Not bad for someone who is meant to have a learning disability.'

I told them I reckoned we had got it the wrong way around. It wasn't that they had a learning disability; I believe we as a society have got a teaching disability. 'Everyone here can learn.' I said. 'If you can learn to walk and talk, you are going to be able to easily learn anything we have got for you. Piece of cake. So who is willing to do their best and really go for it in a big way? Is everyone here willing to forget they have been told you can't learn very well? And promise to stick your hand up if there is something you don't understand or you disagree with. All of you? Great. Let's get on with it, then.'

I walked to the back of the room, passing Bob on his way to the front. 'Yeah, they're all right,' I said. We were away.

These young participants went on to convince me that human beings learn differently and are far more capable than they usually give themselves credit for. Under Bob's brilliant tutelage, every one of the young students was able to take on and demonstrate their new learnings immediately.

As with the Breaking the Cycle, the way we facilitate the learning is more important than the course content. We take a great deal of care, much of which goes unnoticed to the untrained person, to create a learning environment that incorporates the preferred ways people like to learn. Most people learn with all five senses. We use lots of colours and props for those who are more visual learners, music and sound effects for the auditory learners, and hands-on physical activities for the kinaesthetics. This is combined with a curriculum of practical 'how to' skills, such as describing in detail the process of how one learns, or the specifics of building you own self-esteem and confidence – skills that are very useful when you are a young teenager attempting to grapple with the complexities of life.

One critical ingredient in our programs is that, rather than just spoon-feed useful information (let alone spoon-feeding useless information) we describe a concept or a life skill such as how to build trusting relationships, then we set up an experience or several experiences for the learner to check it out for themselves. The result is the learner has a far more relevant understanding of the concept; more often than not, they think they have discovered the learning for themselves, which is far more exciting than listening to a couple of old blokes like Bobby and me.

Once again the wilderness trek proved to be an essential component of our approach. Part of me wishes it wasn't. Not only is it the most expensive component of what we do, but it can get bloody cold out there in midwinter.

The first wilderness trek was really interesting. Most of the young people had only been away from home for one or two nights as part of the orientation to Challenging the Future. The young people weren't the only ones concerned. Some of the young ones had packed enough supplies to survive a nuclear attack. Yes, mothers, the clothing list was there for a reason!

After doing some market research, we had decided to subcontract the wilderness aspect of the program to a non-profit organisation called the Outdoor Education Group, are an excellent company with a solid reputation for delivering great value for money. The trek leader was right out of the 'cool looking wilderness instructor' mould. He introduced himself: 'G'day everybody. My name is Womble and this is my partner Tonya.' I thought for a minute we were on the set of Playschool (just kidding – they were both fantastic to work with). OEG was to be responsible for the physical instruction of the hard skills, like canoeing and setting up tents, and I was to be responsible for maintaining the context of the program, the value base or the 'how we do things.'

In the course room we suggested that, as a way to build trust and increase self esteem, participants should only make agreements they were willing and able to keep. No point making an agreement with your boss if you know you can't keep it, even if it seems the easiest thing to do at the time. Once an agreement is made, keep it. If anyone couldn't keep an agreement, we then taught them a process for cleaning up broken agreements in order to rebuild trust and maintain their personal integrity.

We then asked the staff and participants to sign off on about twenty different agreements for the duration of the program. These agreements were designed to produce maximum benefits for everyone involved. They also kept everyone safe by creating a respectful environment in which they could take risks in their journey of self-discovery.

We went through and explained the agreements one by one. After this, the vast majority of the young people, while not always liking it, were prepared to sign off on it. This process subtly shifts the responsibility for behaviour to the individual, where it ought to be. A good example is the agreement to be on time for every event. This is a useful skill to master if you want to succeed in employment, but equally useful for people to check out the value of their word. From the point where they made that agreement, each individual was held to account. Not in a punitive 'why were you late?' way, which only ensures that people master the art of making excuses or ducking responsibility by blaming someone or something else for their failure to keep their word. Our approach was to ask the latecomer what he or she had made more important than their word on this occasion. This made participants assess their own character and evaluate whether this is a behavioural pattern or just an isolated incident that they can correct and learn from.

Now this is all fine in the warmth and security

of the course room, and when Mum or Dad has made their breakfast and dropped them at the train on time, but out in the bush the value of keeping your word has a whole new dimension. Being up, dressed and ready for 'work' at 6.30 am for the morning meeting was the ideal opportunity for everyone to demonstrate their integrity and responsibility.

We told the staff not to go into rescue mode and wake anyone up. So here we were at precisely 6.30 am by our synchronised watches. 'Count off, one, two, three, four,' right through to sixteen, who was conspicuous by his absence. 'Who is sixteen?' I asked. 'Womble!' the group answered in twelve-part harmony. And up came Womble, beating a hasty return, with the shovel in one hand and the toilet roll in the other. I knew Womble had been up for a good hour, as the roaring fire and cup of tea testified. But early is early, late is late, and on time is on time.

Womble joined the group and said 'Sorry I'm late.' Realising this was a great opportunity, I said, 'So, Womble, what was your agreement about being on time?' Womble looked at me with uncertainty, fear and disbelief. 'To be on time for every event and session.' Great answer, I thought.

'Right, so on this occasion you obviously made something more important than your word,' I continued, with a smile and a nod toward the shovel. 'So tell me this, Womble: are you the sort of person that usually makes agreements only to have other things become more important, or are you someone I can trust to keep their word?'

'You can trust me,' Womble replied with a twinkle.

'Great! Then are you willing to recommit to your time agreement and to do your best?'

'Yes.'

'Then let's give him a hand and get on with the day.'

Had I allowed Womble to just enter the group unchallenged, the integrity of the program would have been undermined. In the staff debrief later, Womble confided that he was initially taken aback and felt quite indignant about my public challenge. But, to his credit, he stepped straight into assuming responsibility and became a great role model for what to do when you slip up or make a mistake.

I also explained to the other staff that if I hadn't challenged Womble we would have forgone the right to challenge anyone else for the rest of the program, and that we would have been ripping off the young people we were there to serve. Incidentally, none of the staff were ever late for a session. As for Womble, he later resigned from OEG to work full-time with Illawarra Workwise.

It was an absolute pleasure to be out with the young people on the program. I was used to hard-arsed attitudes, fragile egos and behaviour that was not exactly a bunch of fun to be around. Now here I was with a dozen young people who were supposed to have learning disabilities, and they were doing great. It took me a couple of days to appreciate, but they were more committed to learning than anyone I had previously worked with.

When I took the brief from Illawarra

Workwise, I was told that people with an intellectual disability could not comprehend abstract concepts. They could only learn lessons that were concrete, and then you needed to allow for many repetitions for the message to get through. But these young people were proof that, regardless of their background or their dis/ability, the appropriate challenge, skills opportunity, and support will produce extraordinary results.

These young people received and demonstrated the abstract concepts we were teaching; they were desperate to do their very best. There were times when I was in awe of what I observed.

Most of the young people in this program would have struggled to pass year 7 or 8 in secondary school. Those who attended mainstream schools were often ostracised as 'dumb'. Yet after being convinced that they were in fact capable learners and taught the process of learning, they were able to absorb up to seven chunks of information, feed it back verbally, then go away and work in small groups to achieve what was required. I don't know about you, but there are times when I struggle to bring home the bread and milk.

The example that springs to mind was when we were teaching the group how to put up their tents for the first time. Think about it. If you had never so much as seen a tent, let alone camped in your own back yard, it is no lightweight task. Yet in no time, using the layered learning methods we had developed, these young people were taking on board what they had to do and verbally feeding back the instructions, following them to the letter and going on to assist those who required help.

The bush provides most of us with opportunities to expand our potential, whether be mastering the complexities of a metho Trangia stove, having to dig a hole to do a poo, or paddling a two-person canoe. This is the recipe for a great learning environment. (Oh, did I mention the weather, fatigue, and having to tolerate tent buddies who throw their stuff everywhere?) Pretty soon, with some deft facilitation, these young people had gained confidence in their learning capability.

We had previously taught them that a useful strategy for learning a new and complex task was to break the task into bite-size, understandable chunks. (Remember how to eat an elephant?) We would go over chunk one again when describing chunk two, then chunks one and two when describing chunk three and so on. Before long the confidence of the individuals and the group was right up there – at times superior to other groups I had worked with.

Even though at times it may of taken a little longer to explain an instruction, there was always a willingness to learn. This was unfamiliar territory for me. I was used to having to battle virtually every step of the way until the young person was sufficiently worn out to be willing to learn thing that these guys would take on straight away. On more than one occasion, I was left pondering who were the ones with the disability.

The pleasure of working with these young people was all mine. I recall Prue, who for the first week or so presented as being so slow and shy. But when she decided it was safe to 'come out', she was unstoppable. During one particularly challenging event, the group had to come up the solution to a predicament we had manufactured for them. The more vocal ones were flapping their gums but not really contributing to the solution, and there was not a lot of 'active listening' going on.

Prue was as quiet as a mouse, but from the back of the group I heard her squeak the very solution the team required to solve their dilemma. Was she heard by any of her team-mates? No. Did she attempt to speak up and make herself heard? No. Prue did what she had always done before: she went back into a world of her own, probably telling herself there was no point saying anything because nobody ever listened to her.

About an hour later, I asked Prue to repeat what she had said earlier. When she repeated her strategy, the whole group looked at her as if to say 'Why didn't you speak up?' There were lessons in this for everyone, including those who believed they were demonstrating leadership qualities by telling everyone to shut up because they had an idea.

I asked Prue how often she had encountered situations where she believed she had something useful to say but no one wanted to listen.

It was obvious from her expression this was not an isolated incident.

I continued, 'So, Prue, when are you going to speak up? It appears to me you don't say much but when you do it is worth listening to. Is that right guys?' I asked the group.

The overwhelming response from her team-mates was 'Yes.'

I reminded her that, as long as she sat there and didn't say anything, we were missing out.

'In a way,' I said, 'you are ripping us off, not to mention yourself. Are you willing to make an agreement with me and your buddies to speak up more? And are you willing to allow me and your buddies to support you in that?'

'Yes,' she said meekly.

'Pardon? I didn't quite get that?'

'Yes.'

'Hello?'

'YES!' she boomed.

'Good on ya girl, atta way.' From that moment on Prue was actively in the game. Whenever we were having a group discussion, we would turn to Prue and ask for her opinion. She was enjoying her newfound celebrity status in the group.

On graduation night Prue's mother came up to me and thanked me for helping her beautiful young daughter to gain confidence. She said she no longer had to speak for Prue when she introduced her to new people. 'It's amazing. For the first time in her life, she initiates conversations with people she doesn't particularly know – and, you know, she really holds her own.' I looked across at Prue's beaming face. Both her mum and I had tears in our eyes.

'You're welcome,' I said. 'The privilege is all mine.' And I meant it.

Among all the great stories from the Challenging the Future programs, there is one more I would like to share. It is about a young guy on the second program who was exceptionally quiet. Now, it's not unusual for young people to go for a few days or sometimes a couple of weeks before they contribute much to the group. Usually, they have discovered that the best way to survive in a group situation is to say nothing, go along with whatever is happening and sneak through to the finish line.

On this program we had a young guy I'll call John. John didn't say much for the first couple of days but as I say, that is not unusual and he certainly wasn't Robinson Crusoe. We challenged him, much as we had Prue, and watched his confidence soar.

Just after the graduation, a woman came up to me and said, 'What have you done to John?'

'Excuse me?' I replied, puzzled.

'What have you done to John?' she repeated.

Feeling a bit indignant, I said 'Nothing. I haven't done anything to John.'

She said, 'No, no, you don't understand. I was his teacher for three years and he did not say a word in that time.'

'Well, he was pretty quiet at the start,' I replied, realising she meant no harm.

'No, you don't understand, he literally did not utter a word in the three years he was in my class. We thought he was mute.'

At this revelation, I was lost for words myself. For the next fifteen minutes I listened to this poor woman talking about the woes and the challenges she had endured teaching in a unit for kids with severe learning difficulties, and all I could think of was I am glad it is not me. I also wondered how I would feel if my child was being taught in such a constrained environment, where teachers were forced to stick with what clearly doesn't work for fear of being sued or sacked. No winners there, I thought. Another case of good people doing very their best in a failing system.

You see, John had just delivered a competent speech before the hundred or so guests, telling everyone how much he had learnt by being on the program and how much he was looking forward to putting his new skills into action in the job he was starting on Monday.

Challenging the Future became the most successful program of its kind in Australia. Among the young people who commence Module Four, which is the equivalent of the Breaking the Cycle program, 90 per cent are still gainfully employed more than six months after graduating. Coles Myer committed 200 jobs across NSW for young people with intellectual disabilities who had completed a Challenging the Future program.

'Yeah, Judy, I reckon it will work.'

As for me, Challenging the Future was a bright spot in a very dark period. It has taken me a good three years to recover from all that occurred with the demise of Breaking the Cycle.

I have struggled to understand the point of what happened. But what doesn't kill you makes you stronger, and I now have a much stronger appreciation for the pain and suffering experienced by so many of the young people I have worked with over the years. I hope that what I have learnt will enhance my work with young people in the future.

*

So what about the future? My hand is up; I am

ready to get back in the game again. 'Play on, no free kick', as they say in the greatest game on earth.

The need for an organisation like Breaking the Cycle has never been greater. The situation facing more and more of our young people is getting significantly worse. I truly believe that we do not have to treat each other in the abysmal ways that we so often do. We do not need to have teenagers feel so useless, unwanted, unloved, and disillusioned with their futures that they take their own lives or resort to destructive behaviours.

It doesn't have to be like that. If nothing else, Breaking the Cycle was proof that, with energy, commitment, resources and will, we as a society can make a difference. We can create solutions that send a different signal to our young. Because that is what it takes. Young people, just like older people, need to feel valued, appreciated, understood and loved for who they are. They need to be able to contribute to society, to feel they are paying their own way. They need to feel wanted and included, and to have a useful part to play in our community, beginning with their families. There is no rocket science here, but there are some strategies that work better than others.

There are many lessons to be learnt from our experience at Breaking the Cycle. If there is a next time, and I hope there is, we will grow at a pace that reflects our resources. Never again would I put a group of people – including my family – under so much financial strain. We would never ever be dependent on a government for our survival. If a government wants to contribute because it believes this is a wise way to spend taxpayers money, then fine, but I would never allow that money to form the core finances of the organisation.

12
So what's next?

I have had many people ask me what I am up to these days and I tell them I am a "Socialprenure", someone who helps people achieve their dreams and goals!

It is my life's purpose and passion to empower people to achieve their life's goals and discover their life's purpose, passion and dreams and goals!

One of the fathers of contemporary personal development Mr. Zig Ziglar says, " If you can dream it, you can achieve it. You will get all you want in life if you help enough other people get what they want"

How I do that is I work with people one to one or at times in teams of one to many to help them identify not just WHAT they want to achieve but to discover WHO they need to become in order to HAVE their life by design and not by default as sadly so many people end up doing.

I then help people to identify an appropriate vehicle that will enable them to achieve the life they have only every dreamt of living...how cool is that!

As many of you realize there are a plethora of opportunities out there and many people try, fail and give up thinking that they are the problem and resign themselves to the 40/40 /40 plan where you work 40 hours a week for 40 years and retire on 40% of your income when the issue isn't the opportunity or even the person, it is a little more detailed than that.

It is true, not all opportunities are equal nor are they all suitable to all people but that is no reason to quit and settle for less than you truly desire for yourself and or your family is it?

Think about this for a moment.

There has never been a better time in the history of the planet to create a life YOU can design, YOU can create and YOU can achieve.

With the advent of the internet, E-Commerce, Affiliate Marketing, Network Marketing, new businesses and so many more incredible opportunities available from which to choose the right pathway or pathways for you.

It is my experience that when you find an opportunity that is aligned with a person's values or authentic self AND the person is mentored, taught and supported to be a PROFESSIONAL in that particular opportunity, some incredible results will follow.

And that is my life's purpose today.

I absolutely love working with people in a mentoring, coaching role to help them dream, achieve and get what they want in all aspects of life from business, health, wealth, relationships, becoming the best parent they can be, becoming the best version of themselves they can be, to fundamentally be happy, satisfied and comfortable within themselves whilst striving to create the life they desire

Dependance Vs Opportunity...

If you have enjoyed reading this book and have a desire for something better or have resonated with any of the teachings and lessons embedded within my story so far and want more from your own life, send me an email to paul@youropportunityknocks.com.au and let us explore together how you can make your dreams a reality over the next 3-5 years together?

Thank you for reading this book and for taking the time out of your busy lives to come with me on my journey so far and I hope you have had as much pleasure and value reading it as I had writing.

Feel free to drop me a line and share what you valued the most?

Namaste

ABOUT THE AUTHOR

Is providing a limited and dwindling welfare system the best we as a society can offer a vast majority of young people in this the lucky country of Australia? (Or Indeed the U.K or U.S.A?)

One man thought not so and went about proving his premise that regardless of their history, their socio economic or educational background if you provide young people with two vital ingredients they will find the third ingredient within themselves to succeed and go from being a tax burden to contributing members of society.

Born in Moss Side, of the toughest areas of Manchester England Paul migrated to Australia as a seven year old and grew up in the working class suburbs of Craigieburn and Broadmeadows in the northern suburbs of Melbourne and his first home was in a Nissan army hut in a migrant camp in Broadmeadows.

After surviving the brutalities of a secondary education at a notorious catholic boarding school in Sunbury, Paul was an early school leaver and attended the school of hard knocks on the streets and at the coalface as a pioneer youth worker in some of the toughest neighborhoods of Melbourne. Sick of witnessing first hand and being at the effect of a failing welfare system Paul created Breaking the Cycle an organization that saw more than 1,200 of some of the toughest kids go from being unemployable to

become contributing members of society with a staggering 97% success rate into jobs when at the time the National average success rate of getting long term unemployed into and staying in jobs was 26%.
Many of the young people were some of the most disadvantaged in the country, drug affected, victims of sexual abuse, homeless, early school leavers, ex-prisoners, living with multiple disabilities who went on to break the cycles which had them trapped in the past and proved what was possible when you provide young people with the opportunity and the know how and support to succeed.

Married to Sharon with two sons Jordan and David, Paul is now on a mission to help other people achieve their goals and break the cycles that may be holding them back.

This is his story.

CONTACT ME

I love getting feedback from my readers, and I would really appreciate you taking a few minutes to send me your comments or to leave me a brief review on my Amazon page.
You can also email me on paul@youropportunityknocks.com.au
Thank you!

www.ingramcontent.com/pod-product-compliance
Lightning Source LLC
Chambersburg PA
CBHW071919290426
44110CB00013B/1416